ON KISSING

Grace Under Pressure: The Emergence of Women in Sport

Fatima: The Autobiography of Fatima Whitbread, with Adrianne Blue

*Faster, Higher, Further: Women's Triumphs and Disasters
at the Olympics*

Queen of the Track: A Biography of Liz McColgan

Martina: The Lives and Times of Martina Navratilova

A Woman's History of Sex (editor)

FOR CHILDREN

Field Events

ON KISSING

Travels in an Intimate Landscape

Adrianne Blue

KODANSHA INTERNATIONAL
New York • Tokyo • London

Kodansha America, Inc.
114 Fifth Avenue, New York, New York 10011, U.S.A.

Kodansha International Ltd.
17-14 Otowa 1-chome, Bunkyo-ku, Tokyo 112, Japan

Published in 1997 by Kodansha America, Inc.
Originally published in Great Britain in 1996 by Victor Gollancz,
an imprint of the Cassell Group, London.

Library of Congress Cataloging-in-Publication Data

Blue, Adrianne.
On kissing: travels in an intimate landscape/Adrianne Blue.
p.   cm.
Includes bibliographical references and index.
ISBN 1-56836-173-4 (hardcover: alk. paper)
1. Kissing. I. Title.
GT2640.B58   1997
394—dc21   97-2763

Illustrations by Sarah Symonds

Manufactured in the United States of America on acid-free paper

97 98 99 00 BER/B 10 9 8 7 6 5 4 3 2 1

CONTENTS

ACKNOWLEDGEMENTS

Kissing is about affection and pleasure, and it is with both that I thank the many friends and colleagues who so generously helped over the years that this book has been in progress, especially: Lyn Allison, John Alexander, Merrilyn Crosgrove Blue, Ruby Blue, Duncan Campbell, Jenny Cobb, Tina Davila, Alexandra Erskine, Rob Ferguson, Harriett Gilbert, Madeleine Harmsworth, Ginger Hjelma, Kevin Jackson, Judith Kazantzis, Jane Kirwan, Frank Lazarus, Anne McArthur, Sarah Maitland, James Malpas, Steve Matthews, Joan Minogue, Julia Pascal, Caroline Porter, Janet Rachel, Michèle Roberts, Mimi Sanderson, Michèle Slung, Elizabeth Storey, Mike Thomson, Michael Tintner, Jan Vaux, and my American student interns, Elizabeth Mills Clarke, Max Leitman and Lisa Spierer who performed brilliantly as research assistants.

Of the specialists who helped, I want particularly to mention Gus McGrouther, Annabelle Dytham, and Dawn Starin of University College London, Francis Bordat, Francoise Delphy, and Marie-Claire Pasquier of the University of Paris,

Annie Méjean of CNRS, Rachel Brownstein of Brooklyn College, Jan Fergus of Lehigh University, Sue Henry of the University of Colorado, Louise Barrett of the University of Liverpool, Keith Jacobs of the University of Westminster, and Martin Wyld of the National Gallery.

Libraries and librarians were essential. Thank you to the British Library, the University of London, the New York Public Library, Foxcroft School and the Wellcome Foundation, the newspaper libraries of News International and the *Daily Telegraph*, and the Raynes Institute and the BBC.

Warm thanks to my agent Giles Gordon, to my publisher Liz Knights, to Vicki Harris, Katrina Whone, Gillian Bromley, Alex Huggins and the many others at Gollancz.

PERMISSIONS

Grateful acknowledgement is made for permission to reprint from the following copyrighted material: Lyrics from the song 'The Movies Get You Through' in the musical *A Day in Hollywood, A Night in the Ukraine* by Frank Lazarus and Dick Vosburgh, © 1980 by Frank Lazarus and Dick Vosburgh. Reprinted by permission of the authors. Martin Amis, *London Fields,* copyright © 1989. Reprinted by permission of Random House, London. Paul Auster, *Leviathan.* Copyright © 1992 by Paul Auster. Used by permission of Viking Penguin, a division of Penguin Books USA, Inc. Nicholson Baker, *Vox.* Copyright © 1992 by Nicholson Baker. Reprinted by permission of Melanie Jackson Agency. T. S. Eliot, *Collected Poems 1909–1962.* Reprinted by permission of Faber and Faber Ltd. Irenaus Eibl-Eibesfeldt, *Love and Hate.* Copyright © 1971. By permission of Reed Books, London. Charles S. Evans, *Sleeping Beauty.* Copyright 1919, Heinemann, 1972. By permission of Reed Books. Dian Fossey, *Gorillas in the Mist.* London 1985. By permission of Little, Brown & Co. (UK). Alan

Transported to the Landscape
of the Kiss: An Overview

The few Berbers on the high plateau were nomads. In the hope of meeting some of them, I had chosen to stay behind while my friends climbed the nearby mountain. Except for any strangers I might meet, I would be alone. I soon met a Berber called Brahim who spoke no English and very little French. I spoke very little French. We communicated well, scratching pictures in the ground. While his wife Fatima prepared lunch, I held the baby Yasmine. Their two young sons were tending the sheep. The sun rose higher, the family disappeared inside their tent and eventually I was invited in out of the scorching North African sun. One by one, three men came to visit. Each on entering said, '*Salaam alaikum*', kissed Brahim's cheeks, and hugged him briefly. This was the standard greeting among men. Women were not kissed in public.

But later that day and far from the tent, my host did offer me a kiss. By then I had sat – perhaps too long – in the afternoon sun, my mind fixed on the nuances of kisses of greeting: the cool air kisses of the West, the equally stylized ones I had seen in the tent, the warm kisses between East European presidents. My thoughts now wandered to kisses of love, or lust, a sometime category of love. But that day in the heat of Morocco, the old French proverb, 'Lovers can live on kisses and cool water,' was not put to the test.

There was, though, a kind of consummation. In a flash of interior light, I suddenly saw the link – the kiss continuum – the loop of unbroken meaning which informs every kiss, whether of ritual or love.

Freud long ago recognized that our mother's breast prepares us for our lover's kiss, and more recently anthropologists have grudgingly corroborated the insight, speculating that kiss-feeding, a child-rearing method of the ancient Greeks which hunter–gatherers in the Venezuelan rain forests still practise, is the origin of the erotic kiss. There is, however, I believe, a larger kiss continuum which no one has mapped. Its landscape includes the interconnecting peaks and valleys of the maternal, the placatory, the religious, the metaphysical and the erotic.

A kiss tells the whole story of humankind. The sucking and tonguing involved in feeding from the breast and, somewhat differently, the bottle, are essentially the actions used in kissing. Erotic kissing is mock-suckling. Kissing is mock-feeding of the other, too: it is offering the soft, vulnerable bits of oneself, the lips, the tongue, between the other's teeth, and knowing they are safe.

Both lovers feast in the ideal kiss.

> Let me gulp your kisses, and you gulp mine,
> And with our mouths sip each other's bliss,

the French poet Louise Labé wrote 450 years ago. One feeds and is fed simultaneously.

Every kiss implies the vulnerability, the closeness, the sensuality and the trust that exist between a mother (or mother figure) and her child. It is my theory that a re-enactment of the security and the sensuality of babyhood by both lovers simultaneously constitutes a great part of the emotional and the physical dynamic of erotic kissing. This accounts for the intensity, the pleasure, the sense of connection and the joy.

The power of the kiss as a symbol stems from the fact that not just the kiss of sexual intimacy, but virtually every kiss, partakes of the continuum of meaning. Only billiard balls kiss with no emotional reverberation. The sensuality and the mutually fulfilling interdependence of mother and child give an underlying meaning to all types of kisses and make the kiss one of our most powerful and evocative gestures. The kiss of Judas, the most famous kiss in Western culture, shocks because it betrays the idea of kissing as well as the ideal of trust.

The fabled kisses of star-crossed lovers – Sleeping Beauty and the Prince, Paolo and Francesca, Scarlett and Rhett, Oscar and Bosie, Charles and Diana – have become icons of desire. And many, like Keats, believe kisses are 'slippery blisses'.

Today, when sex has become dangerous again, there is a new romantic consciousness that makes people hesitate, take their time and kiss. Kissing has a very prominent place in the novels and movies of the 1990s, and in our lives. In fact, it is no exaggeration to say that the kiss has reassumed a primacy it has not had since before the invention of penicillin.

What now follows is a full account of my journey into the intellectual territories of many sorts of specialists, some of them at war with each other. Travelling from anthropology to *amour propre*, from biology to Byronic greed, from Catullus to cunnilingus, I have followed the continuum into the huge and varied terrain of the empire of the erotic. En route, I was kissed by a young gorilla in a forest in West Africa and by an ageing ape at the Savoy. Not even this has dampened my passionate interest in kissing. Like Marco Polo, I have returned with wondrous tales and even a little silk.

A NATURAL HISTORY OF KISSING

The lips of even the most macho man are very similar to the lips of the vagina. Both are sensitive frontiers leading into moist, inner territory. The lips, mouth, tongue and teeth are largely androgynous. For all practical purposes, the lips of both sexes are virtually the same; hence kissing is the joining of like and like. During the act of kissing two people communicate as biological equals; it is a sex act which men and women perform with the same apparatus.

But if the mouth were a penis, it would be erect all the time: eating, drinking, talking, kissing. The mouth is a sensory oasis, one set not in the desert but in the Mesopotamia of the body, the face. Like the ancient river valley where early human culture flourished, the face is inundated with information, which flows into it from the senses. As you begin to kiss, you see, hear, smell, touch and taste your lover. When you decide to nibble the inside of your lover's lip, or your beloved's tongue teases yours, messages from the brain are sent to the muscles which execute the action. Your internal telephone network, the nervous system, links the parts of your body via millions of neural impulses.

Kissing is *reveille* for a vast array of hormones, nerves and muscles. It can make the body warm and the genitalia tingle. And the brain, the control centre of the body, is involved in everything you do, from trailing your fingertips languidly across your lover's lips, to thrusting your tongue between them. The old cliché that sex happens in the head has a certain physiological truth. On a map of the brain, the mouth looms larger than the genitalia. Much of the brain's motor centre is dedicated to lip and tongue movements, which require very fine control. Only the hand and fingers, which are also capable of delicate and complicated movements, occupy as much brain space. The genitals take up much less space.

As you kiss passionately and become increasingly sexually excited, your brain instructs your lungs to gasp, your heart to speed up, your salivary glands to go into overdrive. The sensory messages of touch and pressure move very quickly – like a modem sending a message across the sea – so that kissing is immediately pleasurable.

The soft little kisses now give way to more forceful, open-mouthed kisses searching the other's body. As the tongue of one partner probes the other, neural signals rush your spine, pancreas, adrenal glands and pelvic nerve endings into action. Arteries and veins respond to the signals coming from your lips. As you kiss, your feelings, thoughts and fleeting memories of other kisses are nerve messages which travel in rapid bursts. You don't pause to consider precisely where to place the tip of your tongue, when to sigh. You're running on automatic pilot. But if you want to, you can consciously thrust with your tongue, initiating and controlling its movement just as you do when you taste or swallow.

Visible signs of your lover's awakening desire, the sight of his or her naked skin and intent gaze, add to your excitement. So does taste. And so does smell. Pheromones are a powerful factor in desire and the nose, that most sensitive of organs, can distinguish among several thousand different smells: some people can distinguish 10,000. As your blood pressure increases, perhaps doubling, blood rushing to the surface makes your bodies warmer to the touch, you sweat, and sometimes there is a rosy glow, the love flush. Your heart, beating 60 to 80 times a minute at rest, now accelerates to 100, 110, 120, even faster as your excitement heightens. Your arteries are now conveying blood into the organs faster than the veins can ferry it away. Your lips swell, becoming more protruberant. The very same changes occur in your genitals. A woman's labia open and swell. Her clitoris becomes erect. A man's penis becomes engorged, hardening into an erection. This is what anthropologists would call pre-copulatory activity and sexologists would call foreplay; it is what believers in sensuality mean when they think of or speak of or engage in kissing.

Passionate kissing uses up a mere 6.4 calories a minute during the most intense pre-orgasmic stage, but your heart is sprinting. As the intensity increases your pulse continues to race, to about 150 at orgasm, which you can, if you want to, attain by kissing. Or you may prefer to wait.

As your bodies strain against each other, the muscles of your shoulders and those of your back and neck come into use – as may many other muscles.

In this wild symphony of circulatory, hormonal and mus-cular activity, the orchestration includes many neural cad-enzas. Of course you cannot hear these cadenzas. There was, though, once a musical concerto of kisses, a live performance in Paris a dozen or so years ago. Three hundred members of a concert audience volunteered to come on stage, and for ten minutes, keeping time to the conductor's baton, smacked kisses at each other. This live performance, however, gave us less insight into kissing than did Annabelle Dytham's investigations of the dead.

The cadavers are kept in the basement of University College London medical school and are worked on in a room tiled in cold white. The twenty-year-old medical student, a white coat protecting her sweater and jeans, is cutting carefully into the face of a dead septuagenarian. Searching for the key to the anatomy of the lips, she uses her scalpel to cut away muscle, layer by layer. She knows from *Gray's Anatomy* that the lips consist of the two orbicularis orbis muscles, which as everyone knows, or knew, contract into a kiss. But as she dissects first one pair of lips, then another, Annabelle Dytham begins to wonder.

Human individuality is far more than skin deep. No two hearts are exactly alike, no two pairs of lips are identical. After dissecting more than thirty pairs of lips, she can say with confidence that the anatomy books have been economical with the truth. The lips are made of muscle fibres interspersed with elastic tissues copiously supplied with nerves. This was known. But the movement of the lips is more complicated than previously thought. A kiss is not a simple contraction of two muscles; when you pucker your lips to kiss, they are pulled together as though by a series of tightening purse strings. Computer images would soon confirm what Dytham, a junior member of the plastic surgeon Gus McGrouther's team, was uncovering with her knife.

Repaired and reconstructed lips have trouble kissing because not enough has been known about their structure. Therefore, McGrouther, who rebuilds lips, is conducting an intensive investigation of the structures of the lips and the mouth. He seems politely matter of fact until he starts talking about lips. Then his fascination becomes fascinating: 'No one stops to look at sculptures because of their lips. The beauty of the lips is in their movement,' he says. 'Even the lips of the most famous actresses are only beautiful when they are moving.' He and his students watch videos of Billie Whitelaw performing Beckett's eleven-and-a-half-minute, one-woman play *Not I* with the sound off. All you can see is a figure in shadow and the actress's moving mouth.

The McGrouther team made the world's first ever moving picture of what happens beneath the skin when the mouth is in motion. This magnetic resonance image (MRI) of, among others, Annabelle Dytham's lips kissing, reveals the muscles in action. The picture, which is viewed on a computer screen, can be fast-forwarded or watched frame by frame, and even run backwards to see exactly how the muscles move as the purse strings are pulled together. 'This gives us a better understanding of how the face works as a machine,' McGrouther explains.

A kiss is in fact a highly intricate movement. As you kiss deeply, your head leans forward, to avoid each other's noses, you tilt your heads, bringing in your neck and back muscles. The jaw, the only movable bone in the skull, and all thirty-four facial muscles come into play. And if it is quite a kiss, passionate, McGrouther says, 'Every muscle of the body is used; your arms to hold on to one another, your neck and back and shoulder muscles are straining, and so forth.'

It feels electric, and it is. By putting electrodes over people's lips and cheeks and wiring them up, the team tracked the electric currents flowing from the brain along the two nerves that extend fibres to all of the facial muscles during a kiss. One reason a kiss feels so electric is that the lips are crammed with nerves, and electro-chemical activity coming from the brain's facial nerve depot is intense. Another is that the sensitive skin of your lips is far thinner than the outer layer of most skin, and structurally halfway between true skin and the moist mucous membrane lining the inside of the mouth.

The tongue, too, is a tactile organ, full of sensory receptors. Its interlacing muscles enable you to lengthen or shorten it, and to move it in many directions while kissing. Neck and jaw muscles give it greater versatility. The styloglossus muscle in the neck, for example, lets you point the tongue upward. In our culture, a tongue on the tip of the lip is regarded as a lascivious come-on; tongues are, as a rule, kept hidden. Unlike lips.

The ideal shape of a pair of lips is, like the line of a jacket, a matter of fashion. The leading lady of the silent movies, Clara Bow, had lips like a bow. Garbo's were thin. Kissability is in the mind of the beholder. The sultry wet look has been the *dernier cri* for a long time: Marilyn Monroe's lips are not a far cry from Mick Jagger's extraordinary set. Big lips, fleshy. Joan Crawford, Diana Dors and Jane Russell had a not dissimilar look. But cartoonists caricature the British politician Michael Portillo's enormous set: the too-wet look. The puffy lips of Julia Roberts have for quite some time now been in vogue. Known also as 'bee stings' and Paris lips, a lavish pair like those of the star of *Pretty Woman* can be anyone's for a modestly priced collagen implant. But there is no reason to think these lips kiss any better than anyone else's. Kissing is something we are born equipped for and have known how to do since before we were born.

At just six weeks old and half an inch long, a human embryo has a well-defined mouth, with lips and an upper and lower jaw. The tongue begins to sprout, and the seeds of twenty milk teeth are already planted in the gum. An embryo can open its mouth and press its lips together in its third month, although it cannot yet purse them, something a baby will need to know how to do when it suckles. Before birth you developed all the biological equipment needed for sucking, swallowing and rooting, which you used as a baby nursing and use now in kissing. Mechanically speaking, kissing is almost identical to suckling, using the same three reflexes.

In the weeks before birth, foetuses have been recorded sucking their own hands, sometimes so intensely that they develop blisters. At birth, a baby is already programmed to perform sucking actions, and will try to suck immediately. Whether in the Kalahari, Canterbury or Colorado, once a baby takes his first breath, he begins making mouth movements, opening and closing the mouth and twisting the lower jaw. Many Western babies have been observed, and when the Harvard University anthropologists arrived to take down the oral history of the !Kung Bushmen in 1969, Nisa, who lived in the traditional society, told them about her baby's first minutes.

Nisa's people, who call themselves the Zhun/twasi, 'the real people', lived at the edge of the Kalahari Desert. Nisa had no one to help her when she gave birth to her first child in an isolated spot. After the birth, she didn't know what to do, but the baby did: 'I hadn't told anyone when I left the village. After she was born, I sat there; I didn't know what to do. I had no sense. She lay there, moving her arms about, trying to suck on her fingers,' until she found the breast.

Like a one-celled protozoan, a new baby is almost purely a mouth. Life consists primarily of suckling and tasting the world. Fully one-quarter of the size of a baby's body is taken up by his head. In adults, this proportion is halved to one-eighth. If you touch the baby's cheek he turns from side to side and begins searching for the nipple in an urgent way with little, quick, darting movements. This is the rooting reflex. The rooting action can be triggered by the nipple, by the breast, or just by gently stroking the baby's cheek with a finger. The baby's reaction is to turn his head in your direction and to pout his lips. If the mother does this before offering her nipple, the zoologist Desmond Morris says in his book *Babywatching*, the baby is primed for feeding and will take the nipple in its mouth. Try it on a lover. He or she too will pout the lips and turn towards the object of desire.

Just as the mother whose breasts are bare may find that her rooting baby becomes obviously excited, so does the lover. The baby smells its mother; lover smells lover. 'When the baby is rooting, this is the moment to lean forward, lift her onto to the nipple and elicit the sucking reflex,' explains the authority on childbirth Sheila Kitzinger. 'The baby often enjoys first licking the nipple for a time. Then her mouth opens, the mother slips her nipple in and she starts to suck, at first perhaps rather experimentally, but later with growing confidence and savoir faire.'

And not because she is hungry. The baby sucks because that is how babies are made. Quite different from sucking in a drink with a straw, a baby's sucking squeezes the nipple. The baby grips the area around the nipple, which is inserted deep into its mouth, holding it in place between the roof of its mouth and tongue, and sucking rhythmically. (This pressure forces the milk through the nipple.) The same suckling action is used in mouth-to-mouth, tongue-to-tongue, deep kissing. Try sucking your thumb, and you will see what I mean. Better still, try it with a dear friend.

The breast-fed baby gets behind the root of the nipple and chews with the gums, the pressure pushing the milk into the mouth. The bottle-fed baby has to employ a slightly different technique in which the accent is on sucking. The way you kiss may reflect whether you were breast- or bottle-fed. Some Ph.D. student should do a thesis on the differences in kissing technique between the two as adults. To know for sure what makes a child grow up to be a good kisser, though, would take years of probably unethical research. Because it is known that you cannot trust what people say they do, the researcher might have to kiss hundreds of us thoroughly in pre-arranged controlled kiss sequences. Or perhaps it could be done by machine. In the 1930s, Max Factor invented a kissing machine to test his indelible lipsticks because the workers employed for the purpose quickly tired of the job.

Babies need a certain amount of sucking quite apart from their need for milk. Do adolescents and adults need an equivalent amount of kissing? And if we don't get it, do we substitute other mouth behaviours? Talking too much, eating too much? Smoking? Many infants raised in orphanages at the turn of the nineteenth century lost interest in living and died of a disease known as infant marasmus, literally meaning 'wasting away'. They were fed on schedule, not on demand, and were hardly ever kissed, picked up or held. In a grim twentieth-century experiment often mentioned in psychology textbooks, premature infants who were cuddled three times a day thrived, putting on twice as much weight as those who were starved of touch and the emotional message it sends.

The putting of things in the mouth may be an instance of our drive for self-preservation, our drive to survive – the more things you put in your mouth the more likely it is that some of them will be food. But it may also be an instance of our drive to be attached, to be close to some*one* – or, as second best, some*thing*. And it is probably in part our drive to know – which got Adam and Eve into a lot of trouble but has so far saved *homo sapiens* from extinction.

Kissing is an open instinct. To understand what this means we have to go back nearly a hundred years to Pavlov's dogs. Ivan Pavlov won the Nobel Prize for physiology in 1904 for showing that dogs could be conditioned to salivate at the sound of a bell. At first, the bell was sounded in the presence of food; the dogs learned to connect the bell with food. Later, they salivated even if no food was present. Ever since, the Watsonians, the Skinnerians and other experimental psychologists have been amassing data that 'proved' that most human behaviour is learned.

Unlike a primate baby, who functioned on instinct, a human baby was thought to be a clean slate. It sucked the breast, felt pleasure and was conditioned – it *learned* – to 'love' its mother because it was she who provided the pleasure. Not instinct, not love, but rewards and punishments were the gods that controlled human life. This notion of love in response to goodies was known as cupboard love. Its advocates thought psychoanalysis was hokum and argued that human evolution was the triumph of culture/learning/nurture over biology/ instinct/nature.

This controversy between nature and nurture is at last petering out. In 1958, the psychiatrist John Bowlby brought ethology, the then new science founded by Konrad Lorenz, into the argument. Ethology, the study of the behaviour of animals (including humans) in their natural environment, proceeds from the idea that behaviour patterns develop as physical traits do, through evolution by natural selection. Babies didn't need to learn to love their mothers, Bowlby argued; they were genetically programmed to become attached to someone, to their mothers or to some other adult. This tendency to become attached to one person he called 'monotropy'.

Bowlby and his team – who soon became known as attach-ment theorists – observed large numbers of mothers and babies interacting. Attachment, he said, was a human instinct perhaps as important to survival as nutrition and repro-duction. Because our culture's most widespread sexual prac-tice is serial monogamy – a parallel to the baby's attachment, and perhaps a derivative of it – one tends, during an affair or in marriage, to limit one's erotic kissing to the one special person. So, one could add a corollary to Bowlby: that in most adults passionate kissing is monotropic. And probably for the same reason – to foster and maintain attachment.

Like Lorenz, Bowlby thought that the nature or nurture stew was made of red herring. Nearly everything human arose from both nature *and* nurture. This view has become the new orthodoxy; today even a bishop or two upholds it, along with most geneticists. Many activities of higher animals are open instincts, that is, with elements both innate and learned. Kissing is one of them. Unlike the bee's honey dance, a closed instinct which every bee does in the same way every time, kissing is an activity we have a tendency to develop. In animals with open instincts, experience – nurture – counts. Open instincts are genetically programmed outlines that will be filled in by learning. The more complex, the more intelligent creatures are, the more they are programmed in this general way, rather than in full detail. Human singing, caring for children and kissing function in this way. The ability to suckle is there waiting for the switch that will transmute it to kissing.

Soon after a baby begins to suck the breast, he may close his eyes, the better to experience through his other senses, to focus on the warm touch and sweet taste rewards of suckling. Soon, the baby looks up at his mother some of the time, and the bond between mother and baby is repeatedly strengthened by this simultaneous feasting of the eyes and the mouth. For the baby, the breast, often bigger than its head, becomes the world of pleasure – indeed, the world. This is an experience we don't forget. The hero of Arthur Koestler's *Darkness at Noon* thinks fondly of 'snowy breasts fitting into champagne glasses' and the hero of Philip Roth's

The Breast becomes a gargantuan breast which is obsessive in its desire for erotic pleasure. To the writer and music-hall singer Colette, who sometimes performed with one breast bared, the connection between the milk-giving breast and the erotic continued into adult life. In a memoir she recalled a conversation with her wet-nurse: 'Sometimes Adrienne would say to me, laughing: "You, I nourished you with my milk." I would blush so hard that my mother would scan my face to discover the reason for my colour. How was I to conceal from this lucid, steely and threatening gaze the image that tormented me, Adrienne's breast, with its violet, hard nipple?'

What specifically triggers desire varies from person to person: we all have our preferences and fetishes, and some of us, because of physical or emotional damage, may be incapable of arousal. But the ability to respond to sexual stimuli is a universal human characteristic. Five senses communicate messages interpreted as erotic by the brain, and all of the senses may be activated during kissing. Touch is usually the most potent physical means of erotic stimulation.

Like all sexual behaviour, a kiss is the outcome of three interacting forces – biological, psychological and social. Some experts argue that the latter two are manifestations of the biological. But whatever the source of the urge, few would deny that the compulsion to kiss can be as intense as the desire to eat when you are hungry.

It seems quite possible to me that to feel good we may need a certain amount of kissing the way a baby needs a certain amount of suckling. Kissing stimulates endorphins, the natural opiates of the body. Kissing leads to an endorphin high. A mother's kiss may also produce this rush of chemicals in the body. So do running and falling in love, both of which are addictive.

And if you kiss to orgasm, there is a massive release of the hormone oxytocin. Breast-feeding also boosts this hormone. To find out just what oxytocin does, scientists artificially prevented its release in a group of men on the verge of orgasm. The men still had the orgasm, but it did not feel as pleasurable. So, is the intense pleasure of orgasm an oxytocin high? Possibly. More research is needed, though, before we can be sure says the American biologist Simon LeVay in *The Sexual Brain*. Oxytocin is controlled by the endorphin system which is essential to arousal and pleasure.

The exhilaration of infatuation – attraction – seems to be connected to the natural amphetamine PEA, cerebral phenylethylamine, which revs up the brain. The psychiatrist Michael Liebowitz of the New York State Psychiatric Institute argues that we feel this euphoria when the brain is stimulated by PEA. Other chemicals have also been named as factors; but some pieces of the puzzle have yet to be found. In 1995, a scientific study made headlines in the *New York Times* by suggesting that testosterone contributes not just to feelings of aggression, as had been supposed, but to feelings of well-being. Testosterone, the so-called male hormone, which, however, both sexes have in their bodies (women have less), surges as one becomes sexually aroused. Kissing can be a key factor in this benevolent testosterone rush.

Scientists say that kissing may also be a way of exchanging body salts or a way of exchanging sebum, which is produced by the skin glands and is particularly plentiful on the inside of the lips. Sebum may help us in forming relationships with parents and lovers, just as it does some birds. During mating the bird chews food, then kiss-feeds it, pushing the food from its beak into that of the eager prospective mate; they bond and have offspring. But when a bird's sebaceous glands are removed so that there is no sebum, the mate flies off.

Kissing is also good for our teeth. The anticipation of a

kiss increases the flow of saliva in the mouth, giving the teeth a plaque-dispersing bath. When you are kissing or thinking about kissing, your mouth waters just as it does when you think hungrily about a delicious meal. This saliva bath is an important factor in keeping the teeth from rotting. Chewing gum or a fruit pip will also, at a pinch, make the saliva flow, but a kiss a day might keep the dentist away.

It was once thought that the mouth-to-mouth kiss mingled two lovers' souls, the exchange of breath suggesting the spiritual as well as the erotic. What lovers actually mingle is their sensory impressions, sebum and saliva. Perhaps the least sentimental and most graphic literary depiction of a kiss I have ever read is in Hubert Selby Jr's forty-year-old novel *Last Exit to Brooklyn*:

Harry watched her as she unbuttoned his shirt, felt the slight pressure of her fingers. He almost thought about the guys and what they would say if they saw him now; but the thought was easily absorbed by the alcohol and he closed his eyes and enjoyed the closeness of Alberta.

She stayed close to him, resting one hand gently on his shoulder, looking up at him, sliding her hand along his shoulder to his neck, watching his face, his eyes, for any reaction . . .

Her face had a polished wax glow and her long hair was neatly combed . . . He felt Albertas hand on the back of his neck . . . holding his hand on her leg and kissing his neck, his mouth, sliding her tongue into his mouth, searching for his, feeling the bottom of it as Harry curled his tongue back in his mouth, caressing the base of his tongue with hers, Harrys tongue slowly unfolding and lapping against hers . . . letting her saliva drip from the tip of her tongue onto Harrys, squirming as he clutched her leg tightly, almost feeling the drops of spit being absorbed by Harrys mouth, feeling his tongue lunging into her mouth . . . she sucked on his tongue then let him suck on hers, rolling her head with his, moving her hand over his lumpy back; slowly moving her head back and away from his. Lets go to the bedroom, darling. Harry pulled her toward him and sucked on her lips . . . Come on lover. She grabbed him by the prick and led him to the bedroom.

Harry flopped onto the bed and rolled over and kissed her . . .

Note the intensity with which they first look at each other, the pre-kiss. Note the reciprocal movements. It doesn't matter at all that this is a pickup and one of the two is a transvestite, or that it is Harry's first time with a man. This is how one kisses.

THE GEOGRAPHY OF DESIRE

For years it was mistakenly thought that the Japanese don't kiss. Even many Japanese think that kissing was introduced by Europeans. It is not true. A medieval manuscript warns Japanese men against deep kissing during the female orgasm because, at the height of her ecstasy, a woman might accidentally bite off part of her lover's tongue.

As kissing is regarded solely as a delicious way station en route to coitus, in Japan today there is no easy business or social kiss. Kissing is just not something you do in the street. Gloved businessmen bow. Even television news commentators greet the audience with a bow. 'Strangers would not touch with a kendo stick,' says the British writer Tony Parsons who married a Japanese woman. Yuriko and he had been courting for almost two years before he realized that 'the Japanese don't kiss, that is they regard kissing as sexual foreplay.' But he was jet-lagged when he flew into Japan to meet his future in-laws, so Parsons responded to his father-in-law-to-be's bow and polite smile with an attempted hug and kiss. 'We can laugh about it now,' he says.

Lafcadio Hearn, who married a Japanese woman of samurai family and taught at the Imperial University in Tokyo from 1896 to 1903, gave the West its first *Glimpses of Unfamiliar Japan*. 'Kisses and embraces are simply unknown in Japan as tokens of affection,' Lafcadio Hearn wrote, 'if we except the solitary fact that Japanese mothers, like mothers all over the world, lip and hug their little ones betimes. After babyhood, [kissing is] held to be highly *immodest*.' (My italics.) So they did know about it. Affection, he continued, 'is chiefly shown through acts of exquisite courtesy and kindness'.

Except perhaps when they are alone.

'Gestures', explains one cultural historian, 'are in fact mediations which permit the passage from nature to culture, i.e. from the body (gender, sensation) to comportment, the latter being the transmitter of collective mentalities.' Japan is not inscrutable, just discreet. It has its code, as do we.

Reports of non-kissing in other cultures have often proved to be erroneous. Local people, asked about kissing in societies where it was something one didn't talk about to strangers, have responded by saying kissing didn't exist. Or perhaps, like the Trobriand Islanders, they understood kissing to be something other than what the anthropologists demonstrated or described.

The people of the Trobriand Islands were never seen kissing, and they were amused, the anthropologist Bronislaw Malinowski reported in the 1920s, that Westerners found pleasure in pressing closed lips against each other. At first he thought that Trobriand Islanders didn't know how to kiss. Then he discovered they never kiss simply or simply kiss. Instead, two lovers alone in a secluded spot undress and sit or lie down and begin to caress each other, he reports in *The Sexual Life of Savages*. Cheek is rubbed against cheek, mouth against mouth.

Gradually the caress becomes more passionate, and then the mouth is predominantly active; the tongue is sucked, and tongue is rubbed against tongue; they suck each other's lower lips, and the lips will be bitten till blood comes; the saliva is allowed to flow from mouth to mouth. The teeth are used freely, to bite the cheek, to snap at the nose and chin ... In the formulae of love magic, which here as elsewhere abound in over-graphic exaggeration, the expressions, 'drink my blood' and 'pull out my hair' are frequently used. Another element in love making, for which the average European would show even less under-standing [is] the biting off of eyelashes.

Malinowski was convinced that the islanders 'never indulge in erotic caresses as a self-sufficient activity', instead, kissing was 'a stage in love making which covers a long period of time before full bodily union is accomplished.'

Only a few of the African peoples have actually found kissing disgusting. In some societies the practice may have disappeared for cultural reasons of one kind or another, such as the desire to rein in female sexuality which led to the insertion of rings and other mutilating objects in female lips and to the still widespread practices of cli-toridectomy and infibulation. And even in societies which have demurred from kissing people have licked, sucked, rubbed, nipped, blown on or patted their sexual partner's faces.

In a matter-of-fact, common-sense tone, the *Kama Sutra* lists over thirty types of kisses, some of more interest than others: 'If one of the lovers touches the teeth, the tongue, and the palate of the other, with his or her tongue,' says the book's fifth-century Hindu author Vatsyayana, 'it is called the "fighting of the tongue".' The places for kissing include: 'the forehead, the eyes, the cheeks, the throat, the bosom, the breasts, the lips, and the interior of the mouth'; also the joint of the thighs, the arms and the navel.

The word *Kama* means desire, *Sutra* a type of verse, like a sonnet or a limerick. In the Sanskrit sex manual, kissing is categorized into four intensities and four different types. Kisses are moderate, contracted, pressed and soft, according to the different parts of the body which are kissed; and different kinds of kisses are appropriate for different parts of the body. Of the four types of erotic kisses, only the very last, the greatly pressed kiss, might teach us something new. In the 'straight kiss', the lips of two lovers are brought into direct contact with each other. In the 'bent kiss', their heads incline towards each other to effect the kiss. In the 'turned kiss' one of them turns up the face of the other by holding the head and chin, and then kissing. In the 'pressed kiss', the lower lip is pressed with much force. This is best done in a 'greatly pressed kiss' by taking your lover's lower lip between two fingers, and then, after touching it with your tongue, pressing with your lips forcefully.

Vatsyayana suggests a playful little bet as to who will get hold of the lips of the other first. If the woman loses, she should pretend to cry, and turn away from him, pretending to be irked, and demand a second bet. If she loses again, she should appear even more distressed, and when her lover is off his guard or asleep, she should get hold of his lower lip, and hold it firmly in her teeth, and then she should laugh, make a loud noise, or deride him, or dance about, and say whatever she likes in a joking way, moving her eyebrows and rolling her eyes. This is not one of Vatsyayana's better ideas.

The *Kama Sutra*'s golden rule, though, is this: 'Whatever things may be done by one of the lovers to the other, the same should be returned by the other, i.e. if the woman kisses him he should kiss her in return, if she strikes him he should also strike her in return.' Inherent in the book is a kind of equality of sensuality, a mutuality; but Vatsyayana does speak of certain kisses to be performed by men, others by women. 'When a man kisses the upper lip of a woman, while she in return kisses his lower lip, it is called the "kiss of the upper lip". When one of them takes both the lips of the other between his or her own, it is called "a clasping kiss".' This is, he suggests, a good starting point for the fighting of tongues.

Flirtatious kisses can be subtle: A man, seeing a woman, kisses a finger of her hand if she is standing, or a toe if she is sitting. Kissing the child who happens to be sitting on your lap, or a picture, or an image, or figure, in the presence of your lover is flirtatious too. It is called a 'transferred kiss'. Or: When a woman is washing her lover's body, she leans her face on his thigh (as if she were sleepy) so as to inflame his passion.

The kisses for *ingénues* are not undesirable starting points. 'When a girl touches her lover's lips with her tongue, and, having shut her eyes, places her hands on those of her lover, it is called the "touching kiss".' And 'When a girl, setting aside her bashfulness a little, wishes to touch the lip that is pressed into her mouth, and with that object moves her lower lip, but not the upper one, it is called the "throbbing kiss".'

Elsewhere in the East, too, such things were known, as is manifest in the purportedly sixteenth-century *The Perfumed Garden*, by a Tunisian sheik: 'The kiss on the mouth, on the two cheeks, upon the neck, as well as the sucking up of fresh lips, are gifts of God.'

The Latin poet Lucretius (*c.* 95 BC–55 BC) was well aware of the existence of the deep kiss.

They grip, they squeeze, their humid tongues they dart,
As each would force their way t'other's heart.

Ovid (43 BC–AD 17) was equally knowing: 'We tongue-kissed, snuggled.' Flaubert (1821–80) wrote, 'Yes, yes, kiss me, kiss me deep.' Nor is there any reason to suspect that over the centuries the French kiss became a lost art to Westerners, except perhaps in America.

Kinsey, whose report *Sexuality in the Human Male* was published in 1948, found that only a minority of Americans married before the First World War had experienced deep tongue-kissing, known also as French or soul kissing. Had they been too innocent or merely too inhibited to try really kissing? Or did they simply dare not admit to it? Because things seem to have changed quickly. When the Kinsey research team totted up everyone in their sample, they found a different story. Seventy-seven per cent of the well-educated American men interviewed confessed they engaged in deep kissing. Among the less well-educated, men who had left school at about the age of fifteen, the numbers were lower but still sizeable; 40 per cent said they tongue-kissed. Many of the non-kissers said they thought kissing unhygienic. Perhaps it was also too time-consuming. (In the 1940s, men bragged about how quickly they could come, rather than how long they could make lovemaking last.)

Five years later in *Sexuality in the Human Female*, the Kinsey team found that women kissed rather more often than men: 'Deep kissing was in the petting experience of approximately 70 per cent of the females . . . who had not had pre-marital coitus. The incidence, however, rose with increased coital experience, and deep kissing was in the histories of something between 80 and 93 per cent of those who had had coitus before marriage.'

In both German and English, deep kissing with tongues

is known as the French kiss. This is probably due to the same reasoning that led the Greeks to regard fellatio as a Phoenician practice, and the French to call homosexuality 'le vice Anglais'. In the once extremely popular sex manual *Ideal Marriage*, T. Van de Velde says that Maraichin couples, 'sometimes for hours, mutually explore and caress the inside of each other's mouths with their tongues as profoundly as possible'. But the story that tongue-kissing was originated by the Maraichins, inhabitants of a region of Brittany, is surely false. As likely is the possibility that this idea is the outgrowth of a bad French pun; the word 'Maraichins' comes from *marée*, which means a tide that ebbs and flows (as in the fighting of tongues).

The French, who find it hard to imagine erotic kissing which does not probe with tongues, don't mind being credited with originating the practice, and are greatly amused to think that without them, neither Americans nor Britons, nor other Europeans, would know how to kiss.

But kissing is by no means a Western or a modern invention. And romantic love, anthropologists say, exists in 87 per cent of the 168 diverse human cultures they surveyed in 1992. Most likely, romantic love is even more widespread. The Bem–Bem of New Guinea deny they feel it, but girls facing arranged marriages sometimes elope instead with a different man. Most of the peoples of the world kiss. About ninety per cent of humans have convinced anthropologists that they engage in the practice. And it is very hard to be sure that people who don't kiss in public also do not kiss in private.

In regions where the kiss does not seem to be indigenous, it has usually been embraced as willingly as pop music, tee-shirts, and McDonalds. Surely the lives of the Lepcha of Sikkim, the Somali, and the Siriono of South America have been enriched much more by kissing than by the importation of Western junk culture. Along with dissent, in 1991, Beijing

University banned hugging, holding hands, and kissing from campus.

It would be interesting to know if cigarettes, increasingly exported to the Third World, are affecting kissing habits. A report on sexual behaviour in Britain in the 1990s found that smokers and drinkers have more sex. Or say they do. It might be tempting to speculate that orally dependent people kiss more than the rest of us, but perhaps they simply copulate more and get sufficient oral satisfaction from smoking and swirling brandy on the tongue. Or maybe they simply brag more. The best answer to this may be that of the conductor Arturo Toscanini: 'I kissed my first woman and smoked my first cigarette on the same day. I have never had time for tobacco since.'

Beyond childhood, almost no one confuses kissing with reproduction. Nor is the kiss polluted by the sense of shame which in some generations has afflicted the sex act, or by the once-prevalent notion that ejaculation deprives men of vital energy and therefore is debilitating and contrary to the furtherance of civilization. No one thinks kissing *should be* about making babies. Instead of a damaging sub-text, for kissing there is a rich propagandizing tradition.

Kissing has some detractors, but their numbers are small. Nonetheless, it is worth looking at the view of those who seem squeamish about kissing. Not liking kissing does not necessarily presuppose one dislikes copulating. The kissing and feeding one experiences in infancy and childhood, and in adulthood, and the state of one's sinuses or psyche may be factors. To find out how these factors interrelate might take years of rather unconventional research.

The anti-heroine of Fay Weldon's televised *The Life and Loves of A She-Devil*, whom few would want to kiss anyway, clearly feels that most sex acts border on the disgusting.

'Kissing with the tongue for example,' she says. 'Sharing someone's spit.' She makes a face. The Renaissance poet Robert Herrick, who penned many an exuberant celebration of kissing, also wrote *Kisses Loathsome* in which he declared, 'I abhor the slimie kiss.'

In her essay on kissing in *Female Desire*, Rosalind Coward seems to suggest that women don't like kissing – it is something men inflict on them – and that this attitude is congenital rather than a product of experiencing bad kissers. In his short essay on kissing in *On Kissing, Tickling and Being Bored*, the psychiatrist Adam Phillips says, 'Adults tend to have strong, mostly private and embarrassed feelings about kissing' and pretend to think it 'silly or arch to be interested in kisses'. Perhaps he means his patients. My own informal survey turned up no one who suggested kissing silly or arch and only one sexually experienced woman who heartily disliked kissing, although she did like intercourse. But more than one woman in her very early twenties who had not yet had many lovers and perhaps no skilled lovers told me she preferred kissing.

My 'survey', for which I claim no scientific validity – it was conversation over Côtes du Rhone or coffee – did however include three dozen American undergraduates on their junior year abroad in London, the respondents of a British radio phone-in programme, and European, British and American friends, acquaintances and experts of a variety of ages. The youngest person I cornered to talk about kissing was a 21-year-old male Los Angelino, the oldest an 82-year-old woman in Provence.

Only one 21-one-year-old woman made a face at the mention of kissing and called it 'mugging'. Sometimes it is. The men who view kissing less as a pleasure than as an unwelcome amber light on the way to penetration often rev the engine with the same overzealous insensitivity with which they await the changing of a traffic light. Everyone knows that a quick fuck has its place, but it is salutary to remember that the more intense the arousal prior to orgasm, the more exquisite the pleasure of orgasm.

Many of the men I talked to said they were not too particular about which women they went to bed with, but were about which ones they kissed. I was surprised at how prevalent the notion was among men, particularly those in their twenties, that kissing is somehow more about love than coitus is.

In one of the stories in Milan Kundera's collection *Laughable Loves* two lovers playing 'The Hitchhiking Game' pretend they are strangers who have picked each other up.

> She put her arms around him and moved her mouth toward his. He pushed her away and said, 'I only kiss women I love.'
> 'And you don't love me?'
> 'No.'
> 'Whom do you love?'
> 'What's that got to do with you? Strip!'

No matter how strongly one may agree that kissing is more intimate than copulating, it is impossible to say that it has always been or is for everyone. All one can say is that a great many men and women think kissing more intimate, that it feels closer. The word intimacy comes from the Latin *intimus*, inmost, deepest.

Consider: while masturbating, one can imagine one is having sex with someone who is not there. Or one can pretend it is someone other than your partner in your bed; your companion may never know. It is much harder to kiss fantasy lips. It is difficult and for many impossible to kiss properly –

by which I mean improperly (sexily, sensually, well) – without responding to the other. The paradigm of kissing is reciprocity – commingling, mutual incorporation. In the optimal kiss, desire becomes physically and emotionally mutual. The self-absorption one may feel during the high arousal of genital sex, say many, tends not to be there in kissing no matter how high the arousal. The reason that fantasizing you are kissing someone other than the person you actually are kissing is difficult may lie in the very nature of the activity, a close dance of lips and tongues.

I do not claim that kissing is always more intimate than genital sex, or that kissing is better. In the best of circumstances *both* are mutual, intimate, reciprocal and erotic. Whole books have been written on what the word erotic means, but a working definition need not be complicated – the erotic is sexuality, the principal aim of which is not bonding nor reproduction, but pleasure and/or joy.

One more point. Kisses can be stolen from one who sleeps and lips can be pressed against most unwelcoming lips, but the tongue cannot be used to rape the mouth with quite the ease with which the penis can be used to rape the vagina. The penis can be thrust into the unwilling cavity and remain intact and unscathed – the *vagina dentata* is a figment of the imagination. But when the tongue is thrust into the unwilling cavity of the mouth, when mutual passionate intimacy is betrayed, the unwelcome invader can be bitten, even bitten *off*. Or so the aggressor may fear. So it is hard to betray mutual passion in kissing.

Freud's famous remark 'in anatomy is destiny' is still disputed and is in some ways definitely wrong: our futures are *not* entirely dictated by our genitalia. But it could be that in anatomy is *intimacy*. Not only is kissing a joint dance of lips and tongues, but the dance floor is located in the mouth, that sensory oasis of the face. Is it the conjunction of proximity to the face, partnership in an equal dance and mutual penetration that makes kissing so intimate?

It is no accident perhaps that the great love stories, classics that have attained the power of myth, often use the kiss instead of coitus to represent sexual love. It is not just a matter of prim convention, decorum or prudishness. It is not merely because of the notion that sexual intercourse should be private. A key reason why the kiss is an emblem of love, and why it is said prostitutes don't do it (although of course some do), may be that the kiss symbolizes intimacy as well as orgasm.

The issue, however, can never be other than a matter of conjecture, so no matter how strongly one may feel, it may be wisest to take shelter under the canopy of Michel Foucault's argument in *The History of Sexuality*, that there is no timeless truth of sexual experience.

Foucault also gave us another unassailable axiom: that sexual morality is the product of cultural conditions. In the last decade of the nineteenth century, when Sigmund Freud was seeing patients in Vienna, cultural conditions were very constraining. Sex was the dirty little secret of civilized society.

BAD DR FREUD

'Under the pressure of my hands,' Freud says, 'something will flash through your mind, a picture, remember it. It's what we're looking for.' It is 1892 in Vienna. He begins to massage Miss Lucie R's head. 'Well,' he asks, 'what have you seen?'

'Nothing,' sighs the English governess. 'Nothing comes into my mind.'

'Keep looking.' He presses harder. 'There's something there.'

Urged on – bullied? – by Freud, Miss Lucie R begins to see. 'Yes,' she says, 'Now we are all at table, the gentlemen, the French maid, the housekeeper, the children and I.' It is the dining room of the house of the attractive and well-to-do Viennese widower whose children she cares for. 'There is a guest, the chief accountant, an old gentleman, who loves the children like his own grandchildren. Everything is', she sighs, 'the same as usual.'

'Keep on looking.'

'We leave the table. The children go with us to the second floor. As usual.'

'Yes?'

'The children are leaving for bed – yes, there is something – the chief accountant begins to kiss them goodnight, but my master jumps up and shouts at him, "Don't kiss the children!"'

It was customary in Vienna then, as it is in Paris now, for children to present themselves to family friends to be kissed goodnight. But, the governess suddenly remembers, her employer – let's call him Mr I – had also been irate a few months earlier when a woman who had been visiting the family kissed both children goodnight on the lips. He hid his anger until the guest left. Then he began to berate Lucie R. 'He said,' Freud reports, 'that he held her responsible for this kissing, that it was her duty not to tolerate it, and that she was neglecting her duties in allowing *such things.*'

What things? What really was bothering Mr I? Because Freud's key works had not yet been published, it would have been hard for Mr Incest or anyone else to say. The *Three Essays on the Theory of Sexuality*, a short, sharp book of only eighty-six pages, which appeared in a stream of revised editions during the first decade of the century, shocked Freud's contemporaries by proclaiming that the force driving and distorting our hidden unconscious processes was sexual desire.

Although Freud was not in the modern sense a scientist, he was, to use the philosopher Wittgenstein's term, the proposer of a 'new notation' – a new way of seeing. His views led to a loss of innocence that would characterize modern life and refashion our views even of fairy tales. Far from outraging people, Wittgenstein thought, Freud's emphasis on the sexual source of our actions actually caused a pleasurable *frisson* – people liked the idea. Radically chic people, yes. Others, no. In Britain, sexologist Havelock Ellis was charged with obscenity when the first of the seven volumes of his *Studies in the Psychology of Sex* (1897–1928) was published. Ellis, who wrote on kissing himself, was for a time almost a lone voice in Freud's support.

Even though Freud twisted and falsified data in his case studies to give credence to psychoanalysis, which he was in the process of inventing, he made a great leap in our understanding of the kiss, indeed of all sexuality. After Freud, the mutual sexual desire between parent and child could no longer be swept under the Aubusson carpet.

In *The Interpretation of Dreams,* published to mark the dawn of the new century, Freud set out his theory of the Oedipus complex: 'It is the fate of all of us, perhaps, to direct our first sexual impulse towards our mother and our first hatred and our first murderous wish against our father,' of whom we are jealous. It is the shock of recognition that makes Sophocles' play *Oedipus Rex*, in which the King of Thebes unwittingly murders his father and marries his mother, so gripping: 'Every member of the audience was once a budding Oedipus in phantasy, and this dream-fulfilment played out in reality causes everyone to recoil in horror.'

Freud thought infant sexuality bisexual, but since most girls grow up to marry men he (rather half-heartedly) developed a parallel theory for girls. They begin life with mother as the principal focus of interest and love as boys do, Freud said, but their libidinal desire swings to father when they discover that only men possess a penis. Freud's female theory was fuzzy, and Kate Millett was on the right track when she wondered if children didn't instead notice that only women have breasts. Why penis envy, not breast envy? Freud's main point, though, was that all of us experience a grand passion for the breast. In a letter to a friend, he explained, 'I have found love of the mother and jealousy of the father in my own case too, and now believe it to be a general phenomenon of early childhood.'

'As a matter of fact, the new-born baby brings sexuality with it into the world,' the good doctor would insist to the end of his career. And desire was a two-way street: 'The affection shown by the child's parents and those who look after him', Freud says in 'On the Universal Tendency to Debasement in the Sphere of Love', 'seldom fails to betray its erotic nature.'

The oral experiences of infancy were the key, he thought, to all the havoc – and gratification – of our later affairs and relationships: 'There are good reasons why a child sucking at his mother's breast has become the prototype of every relation of love.' Not only was sucking at the breast (or bottle) pleasurable, he said, it was sexually pleasurable. Moreover, it was the genesis of what would eventually become adult kissing. In biological terms, he was certainly right: sucking, we know now, uses the same muscles and movements as kissing.

But Freud was less interested in the mechanics of the body than in the motivations of the mind. He was studying patterns of awareness – something that can't be seen – which is why today some of his categories seem awkward, the work of an intelligent man groping in the dark.

Everyone's first sex object, said the bad Dr Freud, is the breast: 'At a time at which the first beginnings of sexual satisfaction are still linked with the taking of nourishment, the sexual instinct has a sexual object outside of the infant's body in the shape of his mother's breast.' For the baby it was a satisfying encounter: 'No one who has seen a baby sinking back satiated from the breast and falling asleep with flushed cheeks and a blissful smile can escape the reflection that this picture persists as a prototype of the expression of sexual satisfaction in later life.' With a professional recklessness of which he seems to have been unaware, Freud made it impossible to miss his point: 'Sensual sucking [by infants] involves a complete absorption of the attention and leads either to sleep or even to a motor reaction in the nature of an *orgasm*' (my italics).

Nor is it a one-sided pleasure: 'His mother herself regards him with feelings that are derived from her own sexual life: she strokes him, kisses him, rocks him and quite clearly treats him as a substitute for a complete sexual object. A mother would probably be horrified if she were made aware that all her marks of affection were rousing her child's sexual instinct and preparing for its later intensity.' She need not worry, says Freud, because 'She is only fulfilling her task in teaching the child to love.'

Mother and baby – 'the nursing couple', as they would later be called – were absorbed in a great love affair. Few have depicted it so well as the novelist Naomi Mitchison:

By and by he began to give little panting, eager cries of desire for food and the warmth and tenderness that went with it. Erif's breasts answered to the noise with a pleasant hardening, a faint ache waiting to be assuaged. Their tips turned upward and outward, and the centre of the nipple itself grew velvet soft and tender and prepared for the softness of the baby. She unpinned her dress and picked him up and snuggled down over him on to a heap of cushions. He moved his blind, silly mouth from side to side eagerly. For a moment she teased him, withholding herself; then, as she felt the milk in her springing towards him, she let him settle, thrusting her breast deep into the hollow of his mouth, that seized on her with a rhythmic throb of acceptance, deep sucking of lips and tongue and cheeks . . . For a time he was all mouth, then his free arm began to waver and clutch, sometimes her face, sometimes a finger, sometimes grabbing the breast with violent, untender little soft claws. She laughed and caught his eye, and the sucking lips began to curve upward in spite of themselves.

He let go suddenly to laugh, and her breast, released, spurted milk over his face.

Lest anyone misunderstand, Freud put it bluntly: 'The child is an erotic plaything.'

This did not go down well even at the dawn of a new century. In the face of opposition from his colleagues and from the parents themselves, Freud reworked his theory. At first he said several of his patients had been molested by their fathers; later he decided that what his patients were reporting was imagined. Although this half-turn made for an easier life at the time, it has more recently brought Freud into disrepute. He has been accused of falsifying his views because of social and professional pressure. But Freud never renounced his theory of parental erotic desire; only his view that it was always acted out. And even if what his patients told him about being abused sexually by their parents was fantasy, he insisted in *On the History of the Psychoanalytic Movement*, it supported his theory that the child was sexually preoccupied with the parent.

Thumb-sucking, said Freud, in answer to those who doubted the existence of the erotic breast, was a clear-cut example of childhood sensuality: 'There is no question of the purpose of this procedure being the taking of nourishment.' Intuitively, parents understand this when they shove rubber dummies, fingers and other pacifiers into the baby's mouth to quiet him. In Freud's day, dummies seem to have been scarcer; the Freudian baby relied on his own resources: 'A portion of the lip itself, the tongue, or any other part of the skin within reach – even the big toe – may be taken as the object upon which this sucking is carried out.'

All of these objects, Freud argues, are substitutes for the real thing:

> It is clear that the behaviour of a child who indulges in thumb-sucking is determined by a search for some pleasure which has already been experienced and is now remembered. In the simplest case he proceeds to find this satisfaction by sucking rhythmically at some part of the skin or mucous membrane.
>
> It is also easy to guess the occasions on which the child had his first experiences of the pleasures which he is now striving to renew. It was the child's first and most vital activity, his sucking at his mother's breast, or at a substitute for it, that must have familiarized him with this pleasure. The child's lips, in our view, behave like an *erotogenic zone*, and no doubt stimulation by the warm flow of milk is the cause of the pleasurable sensation.

In Freud's view, the kiss was born because the day of reckoning, weaning, eventually arrives. The baby knows how to suck its thumb or your thumb, but finds that much less satisfying than sucking the breast or bottle. 'The inferiority of this second region [the thumb] is among the reasons why at a later date . . . the infant 'seeks the corresponding part – the lips – of another person.'

Freud suggests that the lips will always be second best. The breast, which was so interesting and which initially the infant thought was part of himself, would be better. But what can he do? He compromises: ' "It's a pity I can't kiss myself," he seems to be saying,' Freud concludes, ' "a pity I have lost the breast." '

No. He or she is saying much more.

The infant has known for a long, long time that breast and mother are not part of himself, but external, other. Freud himself calls the breast 'a sexual object'. What the infant or child is in fact saying is: 'It's a pity I have lost my beloved – I yearn for physical and emotional nurturance.' In adulthood we rediscover it. For what is kissing but sucking and nibbling, licking and probing the lips of the beloved, and tasting the nipple of the mouth – the tongue. We love to kiss because kissing was present in our first great affair.

In Freudian terms, Dr Johnson, whose degree was honorary and not medical, was one of the most highly successful oral personalities in history. Hannibal Lecter, the fictional serial murderer of *The Silence of the Lambs*, who was marooned unhappily – 'fixated' – at the slightly later oral–sadistic, biting phase of infant development, was equally successful in his field.

Imagine you are the devoted biographer Boswell sitting opposite Samuel Johnson in an eighteenth-century coffeehouse. Johnson, poet, lexicographer, distinguished man of letters, is slurping his beverage – from morning till night he never seems to be without a cup or dram of something – and talking and talking and talking, exuding a manic energy that is enthralling when it isn't overwhelming. At this moment you forget how annoyingly babyish, how demanding and helplessly dependent Samuel Johnson sometimes permits himself to be. He is a very greedy man, but you admire him, because of his energy, his wit, his erudition – he is a voracious reader – and because he has greedily gathered the choicest morsels of the English language – 40,000 words, illustrated by 114,000 delicious prose examples – into a Dictionary. It is not surprising that to the woman in the Hebrides who 'sat down upon Dr. Johnson's knee, put her hands round his neck, and kissed him,' he said, 'Do it again, and let us see who will tire of it first.'

From birth to about eighteen months, Freud thought, an infant's greatest pleasure is swallowing milk and sucking and biting on the nipple – rubber or flesh. If this phase is gratifying – if baby is held sufficiently and gets enough pleasure from sucking – he will pass happily to the next stage, and then the next after that. But if the oral phase is frustrating, the child remains stuck – his personality in adult life will have an oral character, evident in his dependence, passivity and 'mouth habits,' which include being over-talkative; in extreme cases, logorrhoeic, when words flow like diarrhoea. *Vide* Dr Johnson.

If breast, bottle or mother fails, and baby doesn't get enough satisfaction during the oral–sadistic phase, God help us. Thought by Freud to originate at about eight months and continue to about the eighteenth, the oral–sadistic phase is characterized by the use of the mouth, lips and teeth as sadistic instruments. Poor old Hannibal Lecter's fictional mother didn't give him enough to chew and bite on when he was beginning to feel like an independent person. Unable to express his anger by biting or chewing his mother's breast or the nipple of a bottle sufficiently, he had to enter the pages of literature to find satisfaction.

The case has been made that in every Casanova, contemporary Don Juan or Jack the lad is a needy, orally fixated baby. In *Love and Will,* the psychologist Rollo May makes the plight of the rake seem poignant: 'Don Juan has to perform the act over and over again because he remains forever unsatisfied, quite despite the fact that he is entirely potent and has a technically good orgasm.'

It is amusing, even perhaps instructive, to see how this idea is implicit in Byron's exuberant *Don Juan*, who is exceedingly hungry:

> My wish is quite as wide, but not so bad,
> That womankind had but one rosy mouth,
> To kiss them all at once from North to South.

No matter what, the Byronic Don Juan remains incompletely fed, his sense of self unnourished. He always wants more.

> Their lips drew near, and clung into a kiss;
> A long, long kiss, a kiss of youth and love.
> . . .
> Each kiss a heart-quake – for a kiss's strength,
> I think, it must be reckon'd by its length.

Although popular culture does not hail the equivalent Donna Juanita, women are capable of the same urgent wanderlust, and literature has applauded their adventures. Mary Delarivier Manley (1663–1724), who was Jonathan Swift's successor as editor of the Tory periodical the *Examiner,* created the sexually voracious Charlot, who 'found everything insipid, nothing but the Duke's kisses could relish with her.' Contemporaneous with Casanova (1725–98) was a spate of female seducers in English literature. Most famous is the whorish heroine of John Cleland's *Fanny Hill, or the Memoirs of a Woman of Pleasure* (1748), whose first glimpse of a penis, 'naked, stiff, and erect, that wonderful machine,' shows she was right for the role.

More to the Freudian point are the unhappy, driven women of the Italian movies, who first came to prominence in *L'Avventura* and *La Dolce Vita.* Donna Juanitas, promiscuous women, have more often been pathologized as nymphomaniacs than perceived as figures of glamour. Far better a Don Juan or Don Juanita, though, than Hannibal Lecter who grew up to be one very angry baby.

★   ★   ★

The grand passion for the breast, Freud believed, became a passion for the mother herself: but for the sake of civilization, sublimation and repression of the Oedipus complex was necessary. (Jung named the parallel feelings in girls the Electra complex.) Few acted out the fantasy of family romance to the point of incest and murder in real life, but all had the unconscious wish, which might surface in dreams or in daydreams.

In *Remembrance of Things Past,* a seven-year-old Marcel Proust remembers his mother kissing him goodnight. 'My sole consolation when I went upstairs for the night was that Mamma would come in and kiss me after I was in bed,' begins the famous passage. 'The moment in which I heard her climb the stairs, and then heard the whisper of her blue muslin dress, from which hung tiny tassels of plaited straw, rustling along the double-doored corridor, was for me a moment of the utmost pain because it heralded the moment which was to follow it, when she would have left me and gone downstairs again.'

Sometimes, 'when, after kissing me, she opened the door to go, I yearned to call her back, to say to her "Kiss me just once more".' Instead, he thought of the moment 'when she had bent her loving face down over my bed, and held it out to me like a host for an act of peace – giving communion in which my lips might imbibe her real presence and with it the power to sleep.'

On the evenings when there were visitors, things were different: 'Mamma did not come up to my room.' Instead,

> that fragile and precious kiss which Mamma usually bestowed on me when I was in bed and about to go to sleep had to be transported from the dining-room to my bedroom where I must keep it inviolate all the time it took me to undress, without letting its sweet charm be broken, without letting its volatile essence diffuse itself and

evaporate; and it was precisely on those very evenings when I needed to receive it with tenderness that I was obliged to take it, to snatch it brusquely and in public.

On those evenings,

> I never took my eyes off my mother. I knew . . . that for fear of annoying my father, Mamma would not allow me to kiss her several times in public, as I would have done in my room. And so I promised myself that in the dining-room, as they began to eat and drink and as I felt the hour approach, I would put beforehand into this kiss, which was bound to be so brief and furtive, everything that my own energies could muster, would carefully choose beforehand the exact spot on her cheek where l would imprint it, and would prepare myself so as to be able, thanks to these mental preliminaries, to consecrate the whole of the minute Mamma would grant me to the sensation of her cheek against my lips.

Albert Camus's autobiographical novel *The First Man* depicts a similar longing. When his grandmother sent him off to bed, he 'kissed her first, then his uncle, and last his mother, who gave him a tender, absent-minded kiss, then assumed once more her motionless position, in the shadowy half-light, her gaze lost in the street and the current of life that flowed endlessly below the riverbank where she sat, endlessly, while her son, endlessly, watched her in the shadows with a lump in his throat.'

Stalin's daughter Svetlana recalls: 'My physical memory was that she [my mother] was beautiful and perfumed. She used to stop in the evenings in my bedroom and would probably kiss me and touch me with her hands and then leave. Her fragrance would stay behind.'

In *The Lovers/Les Amants*, the painting by the surrealist Magritte, two lovers kiss although each one's head is wrapped in a shroud. The symbolism of this kiss is haunting: love is blinded; love is impeded – the cloth separates the two; and the spectre of death envelops passion. Magritte's mother drowned herself when he was a child; when she was found, her nightgown covered her head.

The loss and recovery of his mother's kiss appears to have been a key event in Proust's early life. More overtly than in most cases, the resonance of this maternal kiss continued into Proust's adult life, influencing, says the biographer George Painter, affairs with women. Proust, it seems, may not have been entirely homosexual. His younger brother Robert, a surgeon, wrote a textbook on *The Surgery of the Female Genital Organs*. Says Painter: 'It is a subject not entirely foreign to the Marcel who described the naked Albertine asleep.' An affair with Louisa de Mornand, he says, began in the spring of 1904. Very soon after Proust sent her this couplet:

> He who Louisa cannot win
> No refuge has but Onan's sin,

She soon gave him the alternative to sin. 'I feel', Proust said in a letter to her, 'happier than a child who has just been given his first doll.' In memory of his first visit to her bed, he wrote:

> Two mouths united in a kiss,
> Two hearts that are no longer two.
> The bed is blue, the salon red,
> But the azure jewel-case encloses,
> While nothing moves, and nought is said,
> A pearl whose hue is like a rose's.

Their affair, says Painter, was intense for a few months, but had its moments for more than a year, and covered roughly the period when Proust lived with his widowed mother until she died. 'He was arranging for other women, almost before her eyes, to bring him the goodnight kiss she had denied him,' Painter says. During the last year of her life, their roles were reversed. Proust's mother retired early and waited until her son went to her room to kiss her goodnight.

Fathers, too, are the objects of longing, a subject vividly depicted in somewhat over-Freudian glory in the mid-fifties courtroom movie *The Rack* which reappears from time to time on television. Paul Newman plays an army officer who showed heroism on the Korean battlefield but collaborated with the enemy when he became a prisoner of war. There was no physical torture, but the dual mental tortures of extreme isolation and being forced to recall his childhood broke him down.

Part of the testimony Newman is ordered to read aloud at his court martial is the account he was forced to write of his lonely childhood. His mother, often ill, died when he was twelve. His father, a rigidly military colonel, was usually away: 'As long as I can remember' – Newman is barely holding back the tears – 'my father never kissed me, he didn't hold us . . . I can't seem to love anybody now.' That evening, the father seeks him out. As they sit together stiffly talking, manfully trying to hide their emotions, the colonel suddenly takes his adult son in his arms, kissing the top of Newman's head as though he were a child. It is one of the most astonishing kisses in the movies.

Vulgarity has often characterized depiction of father–daughter incest. There is the old hillbilly story about the young man telling his father that the girl he wanted to marry, who lived in the next valley, was a virgin. Unimpressed, the father said, 'If she ain't good enough for her own folks, how do we know she's good enough for us?' The lust between mother and son, which artists have long sensed and portrayed obliquely, has been treated more reverentially.

One reason why the Madonna and Child play such a great part in the history of Western art, and a reason too for the persistence of the cult of the Virgin Mary – Christ's mother and bride – is that it speaks intuitively of our first passionate love. A lack of self-consciousness about desires which today might worry us is apparent in the twelfth-century mosaic at Saint Maria in Trastevere, Rome, where the adult Jesus, who has been crowned king, sits on the throne with his mother beside him as his queen and bride. Before the mythology of Mary and Jesus came that of Venus, the goddess of love, and her son, the dart-throwing god of love Cupid. One of the most famous depictions of the pair, and perhaps the most memorable, is the sixteenth-century painting by Bronzino, *Venus, Cupid, Folly and Time*, in London's National Gallery. In it, oblivious to the people crowding round them, mother and adolescent son, both naked, are joined in an exquisite kiss employing tongues. Like Eve, Venus grasps an apple. Cupid is amorously squeezing his mother's breast. The Victorians vandalized the painting – which has long been repaired – by adding a vine leaf to hide Cupid's flirtatious buttocks and carefully painting out the lascivious tongues. The original of Michelangelo's painting *Venus and Cupid* has been lost, but it is known to us from copies. In it the boy Cupid's foot, resting on his mother's thigh, grazes her *mons veneris*. She is fingering the shaft of one of his arrows, and they are kissing sensually. Other paintings of the pair are not hard to find.

Like Venus and Cupid, in the world's great paintings the Madonna and Child often have eyes only for each other. An early fourteenth-century Madonna and Child of the School

of Giotto now in the Louvre, a painting often said to epitom-
ize the Christian ideal of motherhood, shows the Madonna
looking intently down at her child. Her gaze made me
instantly think of Princess Diana – she of the flirtatious glance.
The boy Jesus, his arms outstretched, is eagerly reaching up
to embrace her. Were it not a religious painting, one could
easily read it as the pregnant moment before a kiss. In
Raphael's *La Belle Jardinière,* also at the Louvre, the baby has
an almost lascivious look. Raphael painted about a dozen
Madonnas during his Florentine period (1504–8), and even
the most circumspect of art historians tends to mention that
his obsession with the subject may have had something to
do with longing for his mother, who died when he was only
eight.

In *Eroticism*, his classic, much-flawed analysis of the subject,
Georges Bataille claimed that violation – the forbidden – is
necessary to the erotic. I don't agree that it is necessary, but
there are times when transgression does lend spice.

Rarely is the deliciousness of contravening taboo seen so
tantalizingly as in the 1930s film *Mata Hari*, where erotic
love is portrayed as the enemy of all that is holy, but the
sub-text is that profaning the Madonna turns sizzling lust
white-hot. Greta Garbo has the title role, that of the alluring
spy. As usual, Garbo's suitor is an upstanding officer, this one
called Alexis, played by Ramon Novarro. He tells the evil
and erotic Mata Hari, 'I love you as one adores sacred things.'

She asks what sacred things.

'God, country, honour, you.'

'I come last?'

'You come first,' Alexis says.

They begin to kiss. Mata Hari, hesitating, preferring less
light, points to a candle, and asks him to put it out. It is the
Madonna's lamp: 'You said I came first.'

He is reluctant to douse the holy lamp: 'I swore to keep it burning. I'll do anything but please don't ask me to do that.'

'I'm going,' Garbo says.

'No!' He rushes to the candle, gazes at Garbo, then at the candle. 'Forgive me,' he says to the Madonna, and blows the candle out. The unseen kiss, a sacrilege, takes the breath away. Note the sound of the words: Mata, Madonna, Mama.

THE BIRDS AND THE BONOBOS

Plutarch tells the story of a young prince of the fourth century BC who fell ill and was wasting away until his physician noticed that he broke into a sweat and flushed every time his stepmother visited the sickroom. The doctor realized that Prince Antiochus had fallen in love with his stepmother, and put it to his father, the emperor of Syria and Babylonia, that if he wanted his son to live, he had better come to some arrangement. The emperor appointed Antiochus king of upper Asia and named his own wife Stratonice as his son's queen.

Had Oedipus so able a physician, we might never have had Sophocles's great play and the terminology of psychoanalytic theory would be rather different.

As for the theory itself, as early as the 1920s the universality of the Oedipus complex came into serious question, anthropologists arguing that non-Western peoples whose family arrangements and practices of child-rearing were different had no such complex. The Oedipus complex – so convincingly present in Proust's masterpiece – was, Freud's critics said, just something nasty that was going on in *fin de siècle* Europe and Freud, a man of his time, had equated his culture with civilization. But even if the Oedipus complex is not *the* script of life, it continues to be the script of a great many people's lives, and possibly always was. Isn't the crux of Hamlet's problem jealousy of his mother's sexual involvement with his uncle (who in his father's absence plays a paternal role)? Shakespeare never tells us how Hamlet got on with his father; probably abysmally.

The feud – it has also been called a flirtation – between the social sciences and psychoanalysis goes on and on. Anyone who is taught the theory of evolution is also taught the standard anti-Freudian swipe, that Freud got things back to front. Writers continue to repeat the charge levelled at Freud a quarter of a century ago by the ethologist Irenaus Eibl-Eibesfeldt in *Love and Hate*:

> Many behaviour patterns which are regarded as typically sexual, such as kissing and caressing, are in origin actually actions of parental care. We remind the reader of this because Sigmund Freud, in a strikingly topsy-turvy interpretation, once observed that a mother would certainly be shocked if she realized how she was lavishing sexual behaviour patterns on her child . . . A mother looks after her children with the actions of parental care; these she also uses to woo her husband.

In other words, as Eibl-Eibesfeldt said in a textbook on *Human Ethology* published nearly twenty years later, 'Freud read the direction of evolution erroneously. Patterns of caressing primarily evolved in the service of parental care and secondarily became incorporated in the repertory of courtship behaviour.'

But as to which really came first, no one can know for sure. I believe neither side is quite right; as I explained in chapter 1, it is my theory that one's babyhood, not one's adulthood, gives rise to these 'patterns'. The sensuality and the mutually fulfilling interdependence of mother and child supply the mechanics and the meaning of a kiss. Erotic kissing is mock-suckling; and simultaneously, it is mock-feeding of the other too. I can't prove it; nor can ethology; and to Freud, whether the chicken or the egg came first wouldn't have mattered greatly. The oft-repeated ethological swipe is designed mainly to show that ethology has a bigger penis than psychoanalysis.

And maybe it does. Psychoanalytic theory was first, but ethology's data are more far-reaching. Both argue that the erotic kiss is derived from feeding of the young, and that the baby's ability to suck is innate. Freud, though, was less coy about infantile and intergenerational sexuality. In societies without our repressions and taboos such sexuality can be very evident.

Among the warlike Yanomami of Venezuela, a father puts in about an hour and a half of affectionate child-care every day, much of it kissing his child – to provide food and pleasure. The Yanomami, who live in the forests near the upper Orinoco, don't hesitate to kiss their baby sons' penises or to suck them to put the child in a better mood. Governesses in Europe and America always knew the trick too. Eibl-Eibesfeldt hastened to assure us that the practice is a matter of good asexual parenting on the part of the Yanomami hunter–gatherers, not of adult sexual gratification. Governesses, however, were not his province.

Yanomami men and women kiss-feed their children mouth-to-mouth, as did the ancient Greeks, and lovers everywhere drink wine and water from each other's mouths. Scientists have also observed the !Kung pressing food from their lips into their children's open mouths, and have seen this kiss-feeding being practised by Papuans and by mothers in some parts of Germany, including regions near the Black Forest. If one actually holds some pre-masticated food between the lips, children only three months old whose mothers have taught them by kiss-feeding them will push their lips and tongues forward to receive the food.

Many animals and birds kiss-feed their young. After a kill, a lioness may carry the great hunks of meat back to her den for her cubs; sometimes it is more efficient for her to swallow the meat and regurgitate it for the cubs. Male lions may do this too. Wolves are even more devoted fathers. They regularly bring back food in chunks or in their stomachs and drop it at the entrance to the den. Chimpanzees not only feed their babies pre-masticated bananas mouth-to-mouth, they sometimes also kiss-feed adults. Orang-utans and gorillas have also been observed kiss-feeding their young.

As a species, Great White Hunters have bad teeth, worse manners, and reek of colonialism. They are stubborn, too. The maverick ethologist Dian Fossey, who spent eighteen years in the high, steep Rwandan brush and mud observing her thirty-five bands of wild mountain gorillas, detested hunters, but she had many obnoxious old *bwana* ways. With her unlicensed pistol and her Cambridge Ph.D., the six-foot-tall Californian whom the locals called Nyiramachabelli, the Lone Woman of the Forest, became a law unto herself, hiring a small army to track poachers in the game reserve and to inflict on them cruel punishments of her own choosing. Fossey got on better with gorillas than with humans. She was the first person to touch a live, full-grown, wild gorilla willingly, and probably the first ever to be kissed by one.

Full-grown males weigh 350 pounds; the females in the vicinity of 250. When she encountered them, Fossey would mimic their gestures and mutter their deep, rumbling naoooooom, a 'contentment vocalization'. In response, the gorillas peeled wild celery stalks and dropped them at her feet. Instead of the angry, violent, chest-thumping brute of legend, Fossey found a shy, sociable, chest-thumping family ape. Fossey knew that the mountain gorillas she was observing recognized her, and although it is impossible to know what was in a gorilla's heart, she believed the gorillas were fond of her. But when she returned to Rwanda after three years away lecturing and studying, she wondered if they would still remember her.

The answer came in a encounter with a group of 250-pound female gorillas and their not-so-diminutive children: 'When I got twenty feet from them I sat down and began making Fossey-style introduction noises – a soft series of rumbles like gorillas make when expressing contentment.' The nearest female, 'Effie glanced my way while chewing on a stalk of celery. She looked away, then did a double-take myopic scrutiny as if not believing her eyes. Then she tossed the celery aside and began walking rapidly toward me.' Another gorilla, Tuck, dropped the baby she was carrying and came close to Fossey, 'resting her weight on her arms so that her face was level with mine and only a few inches away'. They stared at each other for thirty or forty seconds, then Tuck 'lay down beside me . . . and embraced me! . . . embraced me! . . . embraced me! GOD, she did remember.' Effie soon piled on top of them. So did four other female gorillas who recognized Fossey, their babies crowding round, nibbling Fossey with gentle, kiss-like movements of their mouths in what may have been a sign of affection but was certainly a sign of trust.

Ethologists like Fossey spend years in wild places watching the animals. In a sense, they are sanctioned voyeurs who put in long hours noting down precisely what gorillas or gulls –

or humans – do at work and play. Observing kissing is part of documenting the bird or mammal's child-care or mating or appeasement patterns. Sensuality is hard to define scientifically. Goal-oriented – teleological – behaviour is easier to construct. This is one reason why ethologists rarely seem to consider kissing as a sensual end in itself. What they prefer to do is conjecture about the dawn of sexual practices.

Reconstructing the evolutionary history of human sexuality remains, however, more a game than a science. Like chess, it is a cerebral game of educated guesses, based on knowledge of how the individual players on the board may and may not move. The theories of Donald Symons on the evolution of human sexuality, which he published in the late 1970s, are still regarded seriously. *The Evolution of Desire* by David Buss, published in 1994, for example, cites Symons with approval. Symonsites give the male orgasm – which has obvious reproductive and therefore evolutionary consequences – pride of place. The female orgasm, Symons said, was peripheral to evolution and he likened the role of the clitoris in evolution to that of nipples on men; largely vestigial.

The Perfumed Garden seems to have understood female anatomy somewhat better. Here is its description of the vulva: 'God has furnished this object with a mouth, a tongue [the clitoris], two lips; it is like the impression of the hoof of the gazelle in the sands of the desert.' Perhaps erotica does not figure large on scientists' reading lists.

Of course, the clitoris does do something, and female orgasm does have reproductive consequences. A woman who has orgasms will want sex again, now or at another time – increasing her (and his) reproductive chances. And there is empirical evidence for an Upsuck Hypothesis, that orgasms suck up sperm into the upper reaches of the reproductive tract.

In *Anatomy of Love*, the American anthropologist Helen Fisher wondered if Lucy, whose 3.6-million-year-old bones are one of the earliest hominid skeletons ever found, had sex face-to-face. Lucy was not human, but she is part of the human lineage. Fisher hoped she experienced intimacy as well as orgasm: 'in face-to face-coitus, her partners could see her face, whisper, gaze, and pick up nuances of her expressions'. Such intimacy, she says, fostered understanding and the sense of safety some women may need to experience orgasm. There are many who speculate that the female orgasm evolved with face-to-face intercourse. But it ain't necessarily so.

Some Westerners and many Africans go in for rear-entry positions, and there is evidence that a wide range of female mammals – from cats to cattle – have orgasms in this position. Even though face-to-face sex may not be the best position for female orgasm, it is popular, and not just with humans. The most intelligent species of chimpanzee, the bonobos, and some orang-utans go in for it too. The question just begging to be asked is what led to the first face-to-face intercourse?

In this game one can speculate wildly.

I think it was a kiss.

One Saturday night in prehistoric Ethiopia, a human Lucy discovered that she liked kissing Adam – no, let's call him Luke – and our history was changed. It was a Promethean moment, epic. Fire, Prometheus' gift to humanity, unleashed the power of technology. The first erotic kiss unleashed our sensuality. Instead of the perfunctory rear-entry sex common to the other primates, we now discovered the pleasures of face-to-face lovemaking.

But how had we discovered the kiss? Could it have happened this way? To wean her baby, Lucy chewed up some food and pushed it between the baby's lips with her tongue. She and the baby were delighted, and the practice caught on. Then, one day when Lucy was out somewhere gathering, her hungry baby began squalling, and Luke, having seen Lucy do it, kiss-fed it just to stop the noise. He liked it too, and decided to try kiss-feeding out on Lucy. Or perhaps it was baby who made the first move, sucking a parental lip. Or maybe it was a matter of making a virtue of necessity: one prehistoric Saturday afternoon, Luke hurt his leg and couldn't walk to the water's edge to drink. By Saturday night he was so thirsty that Lucy fed him water from her mouth. Their lips touched, then their tongues. After a while, she climbed on top of him and willed him to enter her.

Soon after the first erotic kiss, another phenomenon occurred for the first time. Luke and Lucy fell in love. It started with a kiss. Often, it still does. Perhaps the physical infatuation that we call falling in love is caused by the chemicals released by sexual arousal which I talk about in chapter 2. Perhaps falling in love is merely caused by the pleasure itself and the desire for more pleasure. Some people, I know, fall in love before the first kiss, many don't. Other variations of the story are possible. Either sex may have first tried kissing with a buddy of the same sex, or developed kiss-feeding into erotic kissing with a child. (Probably because of our taboos against sex with children, ethologists shy away from speculating on how kiss-feeding came to be translated into the erotic kiss.) After her first kiss, Lucy sometimes reached orgasm solely by kissing. And sometimes she kissed and kissed without seeking orgasm, bathing languidly in the chemicals of desire.

It is indeed possible that human primates learned to kiss erotically rather as they do in this fanciful tale of Lucy and Luke. On the other hand, humanity may have developed the new tool, kissing, the *tool of intimacy*, one fine day after watching the birds and the bonobos.

★　　★　　★

Bonobos, the slender, dark-furred branch of the chimpanzee family, look remarkably human and deep kiss – with probing tongues. It is possible that erotic kissing and face-to-face sexual intercourse evolved before the first human walked the earth, before our line diverged from that of our closest relatives the chimpanzees about six million years ago. (Or one or the other of us may have reinvented the wheel, that is the French kiss.)

The common chimpanzee is a novice in the sexual arena compared to his more sophisticated bonobo cousin. Common chimpanzees kiss with open mouths, but not with tongues. Bonobos, the most intelligent of our primate cousins, do; and they need little prompting. A new zoo keeper was startled when one of his bonobo charges plunged its tongue into his mouth the first time they met. Bonobos substitute sex for aggression. Their life is female-centred and egalitarian: females run the show.

In the wild and in captivity, bonobos engage in face-to-face sex, and females sometimes rub their sexual swellings against each other. Like the human female's, the bonobo's vaginal opening is frontally directed, facilitating face-to-face rather than rear-entry sex. They have a great variety of sexual positions and sex may be initiated by either partner. Bonobo expert Frans de Waal contrasts their 'impassioned eroticism' to 'the somewhat boring, functional sex of the common chimpanzee', who has little sexual variety in her male-run world. Like most primates, female chimpanzees usually are not attracted or attractive to males except at times when they could become pregnant.

'Bonobos in contrast perform every conceivable variation, as if following the *Kama Sutra*.' The female bonobo has progressed further along the evolutionary road than the chimpanzee and is open to sex most of the time. Just like the human female.

The world's expert on the common chimpanzee, Jane Goodall, sees bonobo life as something akin to paradise: 'The initiation of copulation between a mature male and female is the prerogative of either sex, and the sexual act itself shows a greater variety of positions,' including the female's favourite. 'Finally, male aggression and dominance rivalry is minimal. It sounds like a utopian society.' In captivity, where the common chimpanzee has more leisure time and less need to worry about survival than in the wild, there is rather more sex that will not lead to reproduction. 'Animals are less concerned with the pressures of day-to-day living than in the natural state,' says Goodall, 'and have more time for non-adaptive experimentation.'

The sex life of the bonobo, though, de Waal says, is 'largely divorced' from reproduction, serving many other functions as well. One of them is pleasure, another is the resolution of conflict and tension.

In this bonobos are like common chimpanzees who kiss when they have made a kill and are awaiting their share of the meat. What looks like sadistic pleasure is probably just a way of reducing tension. Reassuring kisses happen on other occasions too: 'During sudden alarms (such as the call of strangers or the sound of passing fishermen) the female often ran to the male and the two embraced and kissed.' In this one can see the continuum functioning: the kiss restores a sense of safety like that felt by the baby at the breast; the sense of co-union becomes one of community. Whenever they are startled or frightened or excited for non-sexual reasons, chimpanzees indulge in this 'contact-seeking behaviour'. If a fight – an unusual event – starts nearby, a male might bend forward and kiss a nearby companion.

The psychoanalyst M. K. Temerlin wrote a book about having a chimpanzee called Lucy in the house. Lucy lived with him for a decade, and he felt her affection was love. If he or his wife were ill and vomiting, Lucy would even rush to the bathroom and attempt to comfort them by putting her arms around them and kissing them. Goodall took the story seriously enough to report it.

When wild chimpanzees meet after a period of separation, they sometimes greet each other by mouth with 'lips pouted forward to barely touch the other or with mouth wide open and pressed against the other.' Goodall also observed that chimpanzees at the Gombe colony in Tanzania, where she began her research in 1960, kiss each other with open mouths when they are excited about food. Goodall's field notes describe two females who, on finding an enormous pile of bananas, fling their arms around each other's necks and press their open mouths at each other's shoulders before they take a bite of the food.

Until recently, humans were thought to have the biggest penises among the apes. But now we know that bonobos are the champions. Since a bonobo can sheath his penis, nothing much is visible most of the time, which may be why it took so long to discover that the bright pink penis of the bonobo is bigger than the human's. 'Certainly relative to body size (and probably absolutely as well) this ape's testicle size and erect penis length surpass those of the average human male,' says de Waal, who measured bonobo sexual arousal in the zoo community.

While penises are not, except in the act of fellatio, the subject of this book, I mention the bonobo penis with more than prurient interest. Normally, males had erections less than 5 per cent of the time, but at feeding time, de Waal found, the bonobo's penises were unsheathed, and by the time they ate, more than 50 per cent had erections. The first erections appeared as soon as the keepers came into sight bearing banana tree sprouts and leafy bundles of branches, peaking when the food was thrown into the animal enclosure. The link between food and sex 'is very close in the bonobo', says de Waal.

Bonobo babies let it be known that they want to be nursed by puckering their lips. Even more interesting is the response of Linda, a bonobo mother who had no milk. When her two-year-old looked at Linda, one of the California bonobos, with the puckered-lip 'pout face', Linda immediately recognized the signal. But because the baby had been reared away from her and then returned, Linda was not lactating. She couldn't nurse her baby. Instead, she went to the fountain and sucked water into her mouth. Then, sitting down in front of her child, she leaned forward with puckering lips. The baby drank from her mouth. It was a water kiss such as human lovers know. In kiss-feeding, as in breast-feeding, one can see survival and sensuality as concurrent drives in both parent and baby.

It is probably no accident that aside from humans, bonobos are not only the sexiest but the most intelligent of the primates. Openness to sex and sensuality, once regarded as part of our shameful animal nature, appear to be an evolutionary advance. It is where the kissing starts – in our adaptation of sexuality into something more than a means of reproduction, in our ability to make it a key to intimacy and pleasure – that we have shown our intelligence.

It can be argued that Luke and Lucy's mythic moment should instead have been a depiction of bonobos discovering deep kissing. But I think humans are more interesting. And, anyway, there are many *homo sapiens*, both male and female, who have yet to make the discoveries that the puzzled hominid couple in our story made.

In the ancient world, as today, it was believed that falling in love often started with a kiss. When Socrates heard that one of his disciples, Critobolus, had kissed a youth of great beauty, he was dismayed: not at the sex of the chosen lover, but at the risk Critobolus had taken of falling in love and becoming a slave to passion. Critobolus, said Socrates, was 'utterly hot-headed and reckless'. He was acting 'as a man who would do a somersault into a ring of knives; as one who would jump into fire'.

Love is one of the universals, but we have been taught it is a recent invention. Because marriage was widely based on social position, because it was often above all a means of controlling property, many scholars concluded that romantic love did not exist until the troubadours began to sing of it in medieval France. But individual sexual love seems to exist in all societies.

The !Kung of the Kalahari Desert had never heard of courtly love when the Harvard anthropologists arrived. They too fell in love. Sitting in the shade of a tree watching two newly-weds playfully chasing each other in the sunshine, one young man agreed with the anthropologist that the pair were very much in love, adding 'for now'. To him, as to Socrates, falling in love was jumping into fire, but it was the desirable fire of passion. 'After a while,' though, he said, 'the fire cools and that's how it stays. Look, after you marry, you sit together by your hut, cooking food and giving it to each other – just as you did when you were growing up in your parents' home. Your wife becomes like your mother and you, her father.'

To ethologists, this is not so bad. The purpose of falling in love, according to most of them, is to promote pair-bonding for reproductive purposes. The chase, they tell us, with woman acting coy, is a way of extending courtship to see if the partner will be a good provider. Oh, come on. It is a fiction that women are coy for instinctual reasons. Many women aren't; and more would be forward if they thought that assertiveness worked as a strategy of courtship. Some young women are not coy and do initiate sex. Many twenty-one-year-old women – even those who are having sexual relations with men – worry that the men will think them cheap or easy. Our mothers used to teach us this. Now it is the anthropologists.

Falling in love – which often begins with a kiss – leads to short-, medium-, and long-term affairs, the last of which we usually refer to as 'marriage'. Marriage has been conventionalized into the norm, but one-night stands are also natural to our species: quick dips, instead of lingering baths in the chemicals of love. For rearing children, one-night stands are of little help; so, more than one anthropologist has suggested, evolution has provided us with innate addictive chemicals that induce bonding, but they last only about eighteen months to four years. Most divorces come after four years: the so-called seven-year itch, they say, is in fact a four-year itch.

If the ethologists are right, and the bonding of falling in love occurred because human young take so long to mature, and a female needed a male to protect her and the baby, then falling in love might be on the way out in the next million or so years – if not worldwide, at least among the well-heeled, the cultural and economic elite of the West. And consider: today many women bring up babies on their own. Or choose not to have children. The more educated the woman, the fewer children she tends to have. And yet it is just those women, unencumbered with children, liberated from economic want, who have the leisure to fall in love and who so often indulge in passionate love affairs – and not just princesses and the daughters of Greek shipping magnates and Hollywood stars. The ethologists' argument that sexual play, sensuality and, by inference, erotic kissing were created by nature to promote pair-bonding so that our cubs would be safe surely is not the whole answer. If that were the case, all the sexiest marriages would be among stay-at-home mothers and their breadwinner husbands; the 1950s Mom or Mum in her apron would be our sexual ideal, and women who need males as providers would be the most likely to fall in love and stay in love. No one can prove that this is so, and few would even argue it.

It is now a truism of ethology that human sexuality has transcended reproductive functions. Sensual pleasure is not a value most ethologists will die for; bonding is. Eibl-Eibesfeldt, who saw bonding as the main usefulness of human sensuality, wrote: 'In animals, the sexual act is exclusively for procreation; in humans it has a supplemental bonding function. This new function, which is specifically human, is as important as the procreative function of sexuality.' Ethologists, though, do not speak in defence of sensuality *qua* sensuality. Poets do.

A CALL TO KISSES

Catullus made a career of extolling pleasure, infatuation, and sexual desire. The Elvis of ancient Rome – vigorous and very direct – Catullus, who wrote bluntly in a colloquial and sometimes coarse Latin, has become classical literature's best-known advocate of kissing.

One of the most fashionable poets of the first-century BC Empire, he became quite a man about Rome, although he was originally a gentleman of Verona. Later poets often used 'kiss' as a code word for coitus, but to Catullus (*c.* 84–54 BC), who called a prick 'a good stiff prick', a kiss was still a kiss. His long poem *Vivamus*/'Live with Me', addressed to a woman with whom he was hopelessly in love, is one of the most celebrated paeans to kissing in the world.

> Kiss me now a
> thousand times and
> still a hundred
> more and then a
> hundred and a

thousand more again
till with so many
hundred thousand
kisses you & I
shall both lose count.

This exhortation to kissing would inspire later generations of classically educated poets to translate or imitate it. But, unfortunately, not immediately. Centuries of tortured Christianity would intervene before poets could again sing openly of erotic love. A millennium and a half after Catullus, Louise Labé (*c.* 1520–66), who sometimes dressed as a man and jousted, wrote a series of passionate sonnets to her lovers. Sonnet XVIII, probably written to the poet Olivier de Magney, begins Catullus-like and then becomes very much Labé's own:

Kiss me more, and kiss me again, and kiss.
Give me one in your physical fashion
Give me one with your distinctive passion
And I will give you four that braise with bliss

The four lines below show that Labé sensed very clearly the reciprocity which I believe to be so very central to kissing. A woman before her time, she demanded equality in life and in love:

Let me gulp your kisses, and you gulp mine,
And with our mouths sip each other's bliss.
Each, both beloved and lover can be
Two lives, I in thee, thee in me

The Dutch poet Johannes Secundus (1511–36) admired

Catullus's arithmetic, as did Shakespeare's rival Ben Jonson. 'The Kisses' of Johannes multiply:

> A hundred hundred kisses,
> A hundred thousand kisses,
> A thousand thousand kisses . . .

In 'To the Same' Ben Jonson (1572–1637) adds his kisses up:

> Kiss againe: no creature comes.
> Kiss, and score up wealthy summes.
> On my lips, thus hardly sundered
> While you breath[e]. First give a hundred,
> Then a thousand, then another
> Hundred, then unto the tother
> Adde a thousand, and so more:
> Till you equall with the store,
> All the grass that Rumney yields,
> Or the sands in Chelsey fields,

Not to be outdone, the greatest lyric poet of the English Renaissance, Robert Herrick, both adds and multiplies his in 'To Anthea: Ah, My Anthea!':

> Give me a kiss, add to that kiss a score;
> Then to that twenty, add a hundred more:
> A thousand to that hundred: so kiss on,
> To make that thousand up a million.
> Treble that million, and when that is done,
> Let's kiss afresh, as when we first begun.

His request 'To Dianame' is more modest and so is his offer, but the spirit is equally wanton:

Give me one kiss
And no more;
If so be, this,
Makes you poor;
To enrich you
I'll restore
For that one, two
Thousand score.

Shakespeare enters this heady commercial whirl in 'Venus and Adonis' (1593):

A thousand kisses buys my heart from me;
And pay them at thy leisure, one by one.
What is ten hundred touches unto thee?
Are they not quickly told, and quickly gone?
Say, for nonpayment that the debt should double,
Is twenty hundred kisses such a trouble?

There is even an echo of the tradition in Antony's sad farewell to Cleopatra:

I am dying, Egypt, dying; only
I here importune death awhile, until
Of many thousand kisses the poor last
I lay upon thy lips, —

Two hundred years later, the professional rake Byron (1788–1824) made sure he got in on the act. Never modest, he would keep kissing and kissing and kissing:

Oh! might I kiss those eyes of fire,
A million scarce would quench desire:
Still would I steep my lips in bliss,

And dwell an age on every kiss;
Nor then my soul should sated be,
Still would I kiss and cling to thee:
Nought should my kiss from thine dissever;
Still would we kiss, and kiss for ever,
E'en though the numbers did exceed
The yellow harvest's countless seed.
To part would be a vain endeavour:
Could I desist? – ah! never – never!

The kissing in poetry would never stop. It simply took a thousand-year detour as poets tried to avoid the gridlock of Christianity.

In the beginning, sex was eminently respectable. The gods of Olympus indulged actively in the sport of love, and the Greeks and Trojans fought a war over it. Few castigated and no one doubted the active sexuality of the female goddesses, many of whom importuned Aphrodite to lend them her girdle which made everyone fall in love with the wearer. In Rome, where Aphrodite was called Venus, the statesman Julius Caesar not only dedicated a temple to her in 46 BC but claimed to be descended from her through Aeneas. There was honour, not shame, in being close to Venus.

The body, seen as an instrument of spirituality in the East, and a welcome instrument of sensuality in pagan Rome, was to Christian theologians a dangerous obstacle to salvation. Before the Christian era, no pagan woman needed to be ashamed of her sexuality. 'But by the fourth century AD,' says the classical scholar Mary Lefkowitz, 'when pagan philosophers had become as ascetic as Christians, the philosopher Hypatia of Alexandria chose to remain a virgin.' When one of her students fell in love with her, instead of showering him with kisses, Hypatia hurled a rag with menstrual blood on it, and said, 'You are in love with this, young man, not with [the Platonic ideal of] the Beautiful.'

In Caesar's and Catullus's Rome, sex had been taken for granted as a human amusement; it was by no means synonymous with sin. Not yet nasty, it was, however, not always nice: 'I do not care for kisses unless I have snatched them in spite of resistance,' says the first-century Roman Martial in *Epigrams*.

In *The Art of Love / Ars amatoria*, Ovid (43 BC–AD 17) advises seducers to hide their premeditation from the seducee. It is when sexual awakening seems like mutual self-discovery that it is most arousing, he explains, one of the excitements being that each is causing – or appears to be causing – what the other feels. Ovid's ribald tales of animated hetero- and homosexual love would delight and instruct centuries of classically educated gentlemen who, unfortunately, often followed *The Art of Love*'s more pernicious advice:

> Kiss, if you can: resistance if she make,
> And will not give you kisses, let her take.
> *Fie, fie, you naughty man*, are words of course;
> She struggles but to be subdued by force.

Ovid's satirical sex manual in verse inspired a long, unlovely tradition of stolen kisses – non-mutual, in effect masturbatory kisses. Stolen kisses are taken without permission or inflicted on the unwilling while he – or more usually she – sleeps. In the ancient myth of Cupid and Psyche, however, it is Psyche who steals the kisses: 'She flung herself panting upon him, desperate with desire, and smothered him in sensual openmouthed kisses; her one fear now being that he would wake too soon.' The nineteenth-century man of letters and man about town Leigh Hunt suggests that this sport's thrill had not diminished in two millennia:

> Stolen sweets are always sweeter,
> Stolen kisses much completer.

Despite the long-held notion, already implicit in Ovid's advice, that when she says yes she means no, poets through the ages have encountered female resistance to stolen kisses. In 1591, Sir Philip Sidney's action evoked wrath:

> And yet my Star, because a sugared kiss
> In sport I suckt, while she asleep did lie:
> Doth lower

Undaunted, the author of 'Astrophel and Stella' told his beloved that she was beautiful when she was angry:

> Thy most kiss-worthy face
> Anger invests with such a lovely grace
> That Anger's self I needs must kiss again.

Ovid – not to mention, almost at random, the Marquis de Sade, Flaubert, Harriet Beecher Stowe, and the book and movie versions of *Gone With the Wind* – assumed that men were willing swimmers but women reluctant waders in the sea of sex. This idea and the suggested remedy – force – applied to kisses and coitus alike would be in favour for a very long time.

Unwilling to accept that some women found sex repugnant because it was dangerous – it might lead to unwanted pregnancy, of which you could easily die – or because the man in question was repulsive, men decided that it was the sexual act itself that women found repellent. Quite possibly too, sex was not very pleasant for many, perhaps even for most women, as until astonishingly recently men not only didn't understand how the female body worked sexually, they often didn't care. Is it surprising, then, that they defined the good woman's sexual pleasure out of existence but assigned a hypersexuality to the whore?

William Acton's textbook on sex *Treatise on the Functions and Disorders of the Reproductive Organs* (1857), which went into its eighth edition in 1894, is by no means the last 'scientific' version of the pervasive double-think which endured well into the twentieth century: 'The majority of women (happily for them) are not much troubled with sexual feelings of any kind . . .' However, by 'loose, or at least, low and vulgar women . . . Any susceptible boy is easily led to believe, whether he is altogether overcome by the siren or not, that she and therefore all women, must have at least as strong passions as himself. Such women however give a very false idea of the condition of female sexual feeling in general.'

In this way, the seemingly mutually exclusive ideas of woman as prey and woman as evil seductress co-existed for centuries. In such a world, many a woman who experienced pleasure would have felt it necessary to pretend she didn't. Instead of faking orgasm, women would have faked indifference. Not knowing they had the possibility of pleasure, they might make no effort to find it. And many would not ever experience any high degree of arousal. I know a number of women whose mothers told them that nice women did not enjoy sex, that only prostitutes did. Earlier generations seem to have believed what their mothers said. Happily, ours didn't.

Oddly, for centuries people would believe simultaneously in two seemingly mutually exclusive ideas. Man was passionately sexual, woman wasn't; in the sport of love he was, as Ovid claimed, the hunter, she the prey. Yet man embodied Right Reason, woman unChristian and unruly Passion, and she was the lascivious temptress, Eve. Distinctions between body and soul, nature and reason placed woman – seen to be bound up in childbirth, breast-feeding, and sex – in the losing camp.

After the fall of the Temple in AD 70, Judaism in retreat had suffered from a hardening of the arteries. The most open minds turned to Christianity, but soon there was a dangerous narrowing. Paul, a convert from Judaism, worried about the yearnings of 'the flesh', but to him the body was not in itself a vessel of sin. To Tertullian (160–225) and to Augustine (354–430), it was. One of the most destructive ideas in the history of Western civilization, Augustine's interpretation of original sin held that not only had God condemned humanity to eternal damnation as a punishment for Adam and Eve's sin of eating the forbidden fruit in the Garden of Eden, but that the guilt was passed on from generation to generation. Woman, Eve, siren, inept wife and whore, was the source of evil. In her *A History of God,* Karen Armstrong sums it up succinctly: 'Woman's only function was the child-bearing which passed the contagion of Original Sin to the next generation, like a venereal disease.' To enjoy sex, whether one was male or female, was to embrace the devil; kissing the devil, something women especially were prone to, would become known as one of the rites of initiation to witchcraft.

How very different life had been before: 'Let him kiss me with the kisses of his mouth: for thy love is better than wine,' begins the Old Testament's vivid account of sexual love, the Song of Songs. The reply is equally eager: 'How much better is thy love than wine.' Jewish law had taught that sex was holy and that woman was blessed by God. Sexual happiness, far from being forbidden, was virtually a duty. The Koran taught that man and woman were created of a single soul. Far from being denigrated, to Islam the erotic pleasures of marriage were a foretaste of paradise. But Christianity demonized both women and sex.

'You are the devil's gateway,' Tertullian wrote of woman,

beginning the unsavoury discourse. 'You are the unsealer of that forbidden tree.' That gateway may symbolically be Eve's vagina and the unsealed tree Adam's engorged penis; but according to the biblical story in Genesis, the devil's gateway is also Eve's mouth. 'Of the fruit of the tree which is in the midst of the garden, God hath said, Ye shall not eat of it, neither shall ye touch it, lest ye die.' The geography of the tree suggests an anatomical centre; one mouth or the other. And the admonition is against touching or eating. Is it a warning against masturbation, fucking, fellatio, cunnilingus, or kissing? Whichever it is – perhaps all – it is a warning of perilous consequences. But the serpent convinces Eve otherwise: 'And when the woman saw that the tree was pleasant to the eyes, and a tree to be desired to make one wise, she took of the fruit thereof, and did eat, and gave also unto her husband with her; and he did eat.'

Investigating the matter, God asks Adam: 'Hast thou eaten of the tree, whereof I commanded thee that thou shouldest not eat? And the man said, The woman whom thou gavest to be with me, she gave me of the tree, and I did eat.' Like a child, tell-tale Adam blames Eve. Bad Mama Eve fed baby something naughty. But how? Did she kiss-feed Adam the fruit of the tree of knowledge, biting off a bit and placing it in his mouth?

The tale in the Bible is brief. If it went into the sort of detail we expect in our literature these days, it might depict not just the fall from innocence, but the birth of sensuality. Exactly what the forbidden fruit of the Tree of Knowledge was has been open to many interpretations. Was the sin that of the first kiss, the tasting of the other? Or was it the first copulation? Or is it, as some have said, that sex was OK with God as long as we did it his way and with our eyes closed?

The Christian antagonism to sex was contagious. Soon both Jewish and Christian theologians were writing tortured treatises explaining that the Song of Songs was actually about the spiritual marriage of man and God (an interpretation that is still sometimes preached). Such is human nature, though, that even the most Christian of writers would manage to infuse their paeans to spirituality with a certain sensuousness, and, after a little finagling, with lust. But first, kissing would be turned to some strange uses.

WAILS AND WILES OF ECSTASY

One day in the thirteenth century, a sort of medieval young Etonian, a preppie, happened to pass a leper in the road, and on impulse got down off his horse, approached the leper, and kissed him. Lepers were feared pariahs, considered horribly unclean, and leprosy, then incurable, was thought to be extremely contagious. Bestowing something so intimate as a kiss on a leper was a form of self-flagellation, one that might leave more permanent marks than the whip. The nice young man's relatives no doubt were furious. But there was nothing they could do about it. He perversely took a vow of poverty and grew up to be St Francis of Assisi.

St Julian Hospitator was much less reckless. When his turn came to kiss a pustulating leper, the kiss was not a voluntary, impetuous show of human warmth. It was something rather more awful: an acquiescence to a repugnant and outrageous demand for physical warmth. It is a kiss which ices the modern heart.

The compliant Julian's story is depicted in thirty scenes of stained glass at Rouen Cathedral and in Jacopo da Voragine's twelfth-century bestseller *The Golden Legend*. The best version is by the author of *Madame Bovary*, Gustave Flaubert.

The story begins like the fairy tale 'Sleeping Beauty' with the birth of a long-awaited child to the lord and lady of a remote and tranquil castle. The curse put upon the child takes the form of two prophecies. 'Rejoice, mother, for your son shall be a saint,' an old hermit says. A gypsy beggar tells the father that the boy will achieve great military glory. These are the dreams each parent has for the son.

The boy is on his knees in church when he is overcome by a desire to kill and kill and kill and rushes off to hunt: 'He came home in the middle of the night, covered with blood and mud, with thorns in his hair, and smelling of wild beasts which he was beginning to resemble. When his mother kissed him, he submitted coldly.' This reluctance to receive the maternal kiss shows just how monstrous, how like a beast, he has become. Not long after, Julian massacres a forestful of animals and receives a dying stag's curse: 'You will kill your father and mother.'

He tries to flee his fate, becomes a famous general elsewhere, and is given an emperor's daughter: 'every day a crowd passed before him, genuflecting and kissing his hands in the Eastern manner'. The monster Julian who shrank from the maternal kiss, a stylized metaphor for love, has no trouble accepting the crowds' kisses, which are metaphors for the general Julian's power.

Returning home from battle unexpectedly late one night, Julian finds a man beside his wife in bed. In a rage, he kills them both, only to find out that the parents he hasn't seen in years had arrived in his absence, and his wife had given them the best bed in the house.

In penance, Julian again flees and becomes a lowly ferryman, risking his life on a treacherous river and charging no fee. In a terrible storm, he ferries a leper whose nose is eaten away and whose body is covered with hideous running sores. Undaunted, Julian gives him food: 'When he had finished the meal, the table, the bowl, and the handle of the knife bore the same marks that could be seen on his body.' Then the man says he is cold, and Julian lights a fire, but the leper demands more: 'I am dying! Come closer; warm me! No, not with your hands, with your whole body!'

The request gives us pause, but not the saint-to-be: 'Julian stretched himself out on top of him, mouth to mouth, breast to breast. Then the leper clasped him in his arms.' And the two rose to heaven.

In the traditional story the leper precedes Julian to Heaven; in the Flaubertian apotheosis, the leper carries him aloft.

When Flaubert's story was published in 1877, critics said it was very like a stained glass window – the characters were two-dimensional and the style of the narrative flat. But the critic Jules LeMaitre, a friend of Flaubert, called Julian's lust for blood and God 'wonderfully symbolic of the Middle Ages'. The final kiss is particularly medieval. It is a self-abnegation that takes the breath away. Dragon-kissing, as we will see, was one of knighthood's specialities, and kisses of enlightenment exist in other traditions, but leper-kissing epitomizes Christian masochism.

Ostentatious leper-kissing became fashionable among medieval ascetics and the religious nobility. Knights in Jerusalem paused from the slaughter of infidels to kiss the lesions of the Holy Land's lepers, whose suffering was envied because suffering could bring you closer to Christ. Eleanor of Aquitaine (1122–1204) indulged in leper-kissing. What better titillation and proof of humility than kissing the dregs of the earth whom sexual licentiousness – erroneously believed to be the cause of the disease – had marked? What better way of hiding forbidden erotic longings than in choosing to make one's body untouchable? Self-betrayal inflicted with a kiss.

Nonetheless, from time to time there were leper pogroms, some of them by Church edict. Leper-kissing reached its apogee in the twelfth and thirteenth centuries. But by then witch-hunting was already becoming the next fashionable religious titillation.

Witches' souls were initiated into the rites of the devil by kisses. As Pope Gregory IX explained in a letter to King Henry of Germany in 1232, prospective witches first suck a toad's mouth and tongue, then kiss its nether region, then kiss a mysterious being whose face is more dead than alive. After that there is a feast at which a black cat with its tail erect walks backwards, and the novices kiss its nether parts too. Then the lights go out, 'and those present indulge in the most loathsome sexuality, having no regard to gender'.

A French witch named Anne Marie de Georgel confessed to the Inquisition in Toulouse that while she was doing the washing on a hill outside of the village, a devil arrived and converted her by 'blowing into her mouth'.

In 1486 came the handbook for inquisitors, *Malleus maleficarum* or *Hammer of the Witches*. The *Malleus* explained that 'All witchcraft comes from carnal lust, which in women is insatiable,' but also noted that in most cases, if not all cases, the demon's penis was painfully large and the copulation excruciating. Perhaps the only pleasure of witchcraft *was* kissing. The reason women so easily succumbed to the devil was that they were weak in mind and body and had 'slippery tongues'. Written by two Dominican friars and endorsed by Pope Innocent VIII, the advice of the *Malleus* on what to look for was widely followed during the frenzied two-century-long witch-hunt that now ensued – not in the Dark Ages, but at the very time that scientific discovery and artistic creation were otherwise bringing about a Renaissance.

Botticelli's painting *The Birth of Venus*, commissioned for the villa of the great patron Lorenzo de'Medici, was completed the very year that the *Malleus* was published.

In the *City of God*, which took thirteen years to write (413–26), Augustine had conceded that sex in marriage was not sinful if the object was to beget children and there was no pleasure involved. 'This lawful act of nature is (from our first parents) accompanied with our penal shame.' That is why we traditionally do it in the dark. Erotic kissing, having no reproductive function, had come to be understood as an activity of witches and demons.

What was acceptable was the *pax,* the Christian kiss of greeting and the liturgical kiss of the Mass. It was a kiss on the lips – an *osculum oris* – in some rites well into the Middle Ages, but the *pax* was eventually reduced to a mild embrace, sometimes accompanied by the touching of cheeks. By the High Middle Ages, only the high clergy or nobles kissed during the *pax*. In the thirteenth century, first in England then on the European continent, a plaque with a painted or graven image of Christ was introduced into the liturgy. Like the Torah, which is carried through the synagogue and kissed by members of the congregation, this *pax* board, called in Latin *osculatorium*, could be kissed by everyone, and the laity once again could participate in the kiss of peace.

In a highly repressed society, the act of taking communion, the imbibing of the public body and blood, would have infused the Mass with a passionate intensity. The approach of the hands, the wafer to the lips, in the mouth, on the tongue, would have thrilled. And it suited all present – as it still does some Christian fundamentalist sects today – to interpret the tremors of the body, the fainting away, the bliss, as emblems of the love of God. Until the late twentieth century, when for a while blasphemy became an industry, few would dare to speak openly of the latent eroticism of the Mass.

Proust did, comparing the soul kiss of Albertine to receiving communion:

> It was Albertine's turn to bid me goodnight by kissing me on both sides of my neck; her hair caressed me like a wing with sharp sweet feathers. As incomparable one to the other as these two kisses of peace were, Albertine slipped into my mouth, bestowing on me the gift of her tongue, like a gift of the Holy Spirit, giving me thus the viaticum, and leaving me with a store of tranquillity almost as sweet as did my mother when she used to place her lips on my brow in the evening at Combrey.

This mention of the kiss of peace, the viaticum, and the Holy Spirit has been excised from the established text of *Remembrance of Things Past*: the passage quoted here is from a variant edition. Many a medieval comparison was probably consigned to the flames, although the twelfth-century lover Heloïse's erotic thoughts during Mass do survive – as do prurient notions about what goes on between priests and nuns. The twentieth century's first major artist to produce a large body of unabashedly erotic work, Egon Schiele (1890–1918), painted *A Cardinal Embracing a Nun* in 1912. Both figures are on their knees in mock prayer; the nun seems tentative – guilty? – about the impending kiss. Schiele's works landed him in prison on charges of pornography.

Medieval blasphemers faced worse. If the only justification of heterosexual sex was procreation, then kissing was wanton and unnatural, as were oral sex and anal sex, all aspects of homosexuality and any intercourse for pleasure. But not everyone followed the rules. Even among theologians, theology was one thing, daily life quite another.

★　　★　　★

The Emperor Charlemagne's friend and spiritual adviser Alcuin, an eighth-century Englishman who became the Archbishop of Tours, wrote in a love letter: 'I think of your love and friendship with such sweet memories, reverend bishop, that I long for that lovely time when I may be able to clutch the neck of your sweetness with the finger of my desires . . . how I would sink in your embraces . . . how I would cover, with tightly pressed lips, not only your eyes, ears, and mouth, but also your very fingers and toes, not once but many a time.'

Alcuin was one of many who avoided the temptation of women by acceding to the temptation of men. Homosexual friendships, which had been widespread in classical Greece and Rome, were also popular among the Christian clergy, who could cite biblical authority in the model of Jonathan and David: 'My brother Jonathan: very pleasant hast thou been unto me: thy love to me was wonderful, passing the love of women' (2 Samuel 1: 26).

Centuries of churchmen and churchwomen found solace in such passionate friendships, called *amiciae* in Latin. There is no sense of sin in Alcuin's love letter or in similar documents. A twelfth-century German nun wrote to her female lover:

When I recall the kisses you gave me,
And how with tender words you caressed my little
   breasts,
I want to die
Because I cannot see you.
Come home, sweet love!

Heterosexuality *was* possible in the Church, however, so long as you stayed in the closet. The theologian Peter Abelard (1079–1142), who was to become one of history's fabled heterosexual lovers, extolled the passion of *amiciae*:

> More than a brother to me, Jonathan . . .
> One soul with me.

His famous affair was with Heloïse. She was, it pleased Abelard to note, more than twenty years younger than he, and as intelligent as she was (for the moment) innocent. Pretty, too: 'tall and well-proportioned [with] very white teeth'. Heloïse (c.1100–c.1163) was the niece of a local canon; Abelard the arrogant director of the Notre Dame cloister school: 'So distinguished was my name, and I possessed such advantages of youth and comeliness,' he writes in *Historia calamitatum*, 'that no matter what woman I might favour with my love, I dreaded rejection of none.' He arranged to board at the canon's household, and in return give lessons to Heloïse, for whom he was 'on fire with passion'. 'Her studies allowed us to withdraw in private, as love craved. With our books open before us, more talk of love than books passed between us, and more kissing than learning.' When he discovered them, Heloïse's uncle castrated Abelard, who had already sent Heloïse off to become a nun. Eventually she became a prioress, but found it hard to repent of her sexual sins and wrote Abelard what must have been a less than consoling letter:

> Even during the celebration of the Mass, when our prayers should be purer, lewd visions of those pleasures take such a hold upon my unhappy soul that my thoughts are on wantonness instead of prayers. [That] single wound of the body by freeing you from such torments has healed many wounds in your soul . . . But for me, youth and passion and experience of the pleasures which were so delightful intensify the torments of the flesh and longings of desire.

In this sort of world – in a culture of tormented arousal – it was high time for a code of adultery. In about 1185

Andreas Capellanus, an accommodating chaplain, and the author of *The Art of Courtly Love/De arte honete amandi*, wrote that pure love, *amor purus*, 'goes so far as the kiss and the embrace and the modest contact with the nude lover, omitting the final solace, for that is not permitted to those who wish to love purely'. His view caught on.

It offered quite a lot, and its sub-text was a promise of more, for it is hard to believe that after the 'modest contact' of kissing one's naked lover, every courtly lover desisted. And if one did desist – it was an exquisite torture. One could wander about the manor suffused with desire and an exaltation of feeling and hormones. Playing this aristocratic game strictly according to the rules had the advantage of avoiding pregnancy. There were other practical benefits: *concubitus sine actu* – caressing without the sex act – joined the souls but left the seed unspilled and therefore did not use up the vital fluids and wither the brain cells (an Aristotelian idea that still lingers). The game of courtly love could be played like a sort of physical chess. The progression of moves in the game – *tener* (holding), *ambrassar* (embracing), *baizar* (kissing) and *manejar* (fondling or caressing) – would stop short of penetration. Of course, unlike chess, love was a game in which one often broke the rules.

Take the case of Lancelot and Guinevere. He was King Arthur's best friend as well as his most famous knight; she, of course, was Arthur's wife. It is no wonder the situation got out of hand, and she was forced to enter a convent, one of the least suitable places even in the medieval world for a woman of Guinevere's temperament. And so she became a paradigm, one of the first of many good women said to have chosen denial before dishonour. But she was much, much bolder than that. Before Guinevere fled Lancelot's kisses, she and he exchanged a great many: 'And the Queen extends her arms to him and, embracing him, presses him tightly against her bosom, drawing him into the bed beside her and showing him every possible satisfaction,' reports the pre-eminent French poet of the twelfth century, Chrétien de Troyes. 'Their sport is so agreeable and sweet, as they kiss and fondle each other, that in truth such a marvellous joy comes over them as was never seen or known.'

The story of Tristan and Iseult was even racier. Yet genera-tions of students have been taught that the basic tenet of medieval romance was look but don't touch. Some were even taught that before the advent of Andreas Capellanus and the troubadours of eleventh- and twelfth-century Provence, there was no such thing as falling in love – indeed, no such thing as romantic love. 'For a long time I believed, following Denis de Rougement and his famous book *Love and the Western World*, that this sentiment was exclusive to our civiliz-ation and that it was born in a definite place and period,' the Nobel laureate Octavio Paz admits in *The Double Flame*. But hominids have been subject to the slings and arrows for eons. Those who have had no contact with Western tradition also fall in love; possibly with fewer problems, for they have been spared our tortured heritage.

And the troubadours' songs of 'pure love' were imported. It was the enemies of the Crusaders, the Moors, who origin-ally sang them. In *An Intimate History of Humanity,* the his-torian Theodore Zeldin finds 'five quite distinct kinds of passionate love' in ancient Araby. Here were the seeds from which the troubadours of the West squeezed their ideas of romance.

Rarely did troubadours sing blatantly of consummated love, and they even spoke of a chastity which could survive any temptation. But even their most devout praises of the Divine Beloved seemed also to allude to some living, breath-ing beloved. And there is often a sense of droll *double entendre*.

The plot of medieval romance, the desirable damsel in

distress who is rescued by the powerful male on horseback, survives, and not just in Westerns. Romance is a fantasy that flows through our culture and titillates through a variety of fanciful tributaries. In the 1990 movie *Pretty Woman*, despite their commercial sexual arrangement the prostitute and the millionaire accidentally fall in love, but the lovers are separated by circumstance and apparently fate. She is a rough diamond; his attention and money transform her into an elegant tiara. At the end, the hero arrives in a chauffeured limousine to rescue her from the dragon of poverty.

In the Middle Ages women were themselves the dragons. The ballad 'The Weddynge of Sr Gawen and Dame Ragnell' tells how when the knight accepts the hideous creature for what she is, she changes into a lovely one. In the fourteenth-century travel book by Sir John Mandeville, Hippocrates' daughter was changed into the 'forme and lykenesse of a gret Dragoun, that is an hundred Fadme of lengthe', and 'schalle so endure in that forme of a Dragoun, unto the tyme that a Knighte come, that is so hardy, that dar come to hire and kisse hire on the Mouthe.'

In *Sir Gawain and the Green Knight*, the great 2,500-line Middle English poem, Gawain wards off not a dragon but the wiles of a beautiful woman. On the first day, while the lord of the castle is out hunting, the lady of the castle gives him one kiss; on the second day two; on the third, three and a girdle which has magical properties. As agreed, each evening Gawain trades the kisses with his host for the animals slain in the hunt but, breaking his word of honour, he holds on to the girdle to protect him in his coming battle with the Green Knight. All ends enigmatically but well, with the Green Knight turning out to be the lord of the manor. He attempts to chop off Gawain's neck, but cuts it only slightly. Because he broke his word and kept the girdle, Gawain gets the nick in the neck but the dishonourable girdle saves his life.

No one quite knows what this particular game of love means. Is it that kisses gird you for battle, that love can save your life? Is it another depiction of the fact that the rules in any game of love are best broken? Gawain speaks ill of the snares of women; but they save him. The intention of the medieval poet, who may have been speaking to two audiences at once is, perhaps intentionally, hard to decipher.

The romance of *Tristan and Iseult* is cynical and bawdy. Tristan and Iseult fall in love when they unknowingly drink the love potion Iseult is supposed to share with her husband-to-be King Mark. Years long, their relationship begins with a kiss. Their love, like that of Lancelot and Guinevere, is fraught with mortal peril. Guinevere is threatened with the stake more than once, and would have been burned if Lancelot's victories in the lists had not repeatedly proved her honour. Adultery endangered more than the soul in those days, but as the alternative was a life of spinning Bayeux tapestries, it is a wonder any lady ever stayed alone in her husband's bed. When wicked barons convince the king that Queen Iseult and Tristan have deceived him, Iseult must defend her honour. Otherwise the good King Mark will throw his wife to the lepers, to a band of them to use and infect as they like, so that she will have a long, lingering horrible death.

Being a woman, Iseult must find a knight willing to fight and kill a wicked baron on her behalf. One eagerly pledges to clear her name: If not, 'May God make me lose my reason . . . and may I never kiss another lovely woman beneath the sheets!'

Finally, Iseult must swear on holy relics that there was nothing untoward between her and Tristan. The crowd assembles at the edge of a bog, over which Tristan, disguised as a leper, carries Iseult, riding piggyback, astride his shoulders. Not a thread of her silk and ermine robes is muddied.

But the wicked barons who, of course, have been telling the truth, fall into the mire. One can see the French tale-teller and his audience laughing at the muddy moral and geographical terrain of the Britons. When all are assembled, Iseult swears that 'No man ever came between my thighs except the leper who carried me on his back across the ford and my husband.' Her reputation is saved; the audience must have shaken with laughter.

Tristan and Iseult, a tale as rambling as a soap opera, has a sharp moral and political edge. It is a barbed critique of that convention in which the king is always right – even though he is a fool and a villain. The story is Celtic in origin and was written down in medieval French in about 1150, but that text has been lost. The two earliest extant versions of the story, one by Thomas, an Anglo-Norman, the other by Beroul, were written about twenty years later. The tale has inspired works in many genres, not the least being Wagner's opera *Tristan and Isolde.*

As in *Romeo and Juliet* and many other later tales of star-crossed lovers, it is the death of the lovers we remember most vividly. Tristan, dying of a war wound, one of the professional hazards of knighthood, sends a message to Iseult to come to him. When a white-sailed ship appears on the horizon, Tristan's spurned wife, whose name is also Iseult, tells him that its sails are black. Black sails are the signal that Iseult the Fair, the one he loves, is not on board. It has been a long, long, love affair; believing it over, unassuaged by marriage, Tristan dies. The ship lands and Iseult runs, her cloak 'random and wild', to Tristan, only to find him dead. In Beroul's version, 'She moved the body a little and lay down by Tristan, beside her friend. She kissed his mouth and his face, and clasped him closely; and so gave up her soul, and died beside him of grief.'

But in the version written by Thomas, Iseult runs up the

street without her cloak, startling the Bretons with her beauty. Then in a long soliloquy she remembers 'our joy, our rapture, and the great sorrow and pain that have been in our loving'. 'You died for my love, and I, love, die of grief, for I could not come in time to heal your wound.' If storm had not delayed her ship, 'I should have reminded you of this and kissed you and embraced you. If I had failed to cure you, then we could have died together.' Iseult 'takes him in her arms and then, lying at full length, she kisses his face and lips and clasps him tightly to her. Then straining body to body, mouth to mouth, she at once renders up her spirit and thus at his side dies of sorrow for her lover.'

Flaubert, who had done his medieval homework, used very similar words in his depiction of the kiss between Julian and the leper: 'Julian stretched himself out on top of him, mouth to mouth, breast to breast.' And they rose to heaven.

Was it perhaps 'the little death' – orgasm – that Iseult experienced instead of or as well as real death? And what about Julian? None of the sexual innuendo would have been lost on the original audience of *Tristan*, who enjoyed the farce and the ecstasy but took it all with a grain of salt. 'To die of love is to love too much,' says the old medieval proverb.

Dante would have disagreed. His quest for the dead Beatrice takes him into the realm of the dead. Dante (1265–1321) purportedly wrote one of the world's greatest love stories for the glory of God. In the *Divine Comedy* – the *Inferno, Purgatory* and *Paradise* – Beatrice, an embodiment of Divine Wisdom, awakens in Dante an intense spiritual love which brings about his salvation. The lesson is that the love of God surpasses all others. Centuries of readers appear to have accepted this explanation at face value, but it is Dante's sinners who have captured their imagination.

In the *Inferno*, Dante meets Paolo and Francesca and by a peculiar poetic alchemy not only transforms them into enduring symbols of love, but makes their single kiss one of the world's most famous. Their sad story appealed to many artists, especially in the nineteenth century when the painter Ingres and the sculptor Rodin depicted the couple. Early movies, too, drew on the story. *Francesca da Rimini: or The Two Brothers* appeared in 1907; four years later came *Dante's Inferno*, a five-reel, Italian-made, hour-and-a-half-long feature.

Dante's encounter with the lovers takes place in the whirlwind of the second circle of Hell. His guide, the Latin poet Virgil, points out many other famous lovers, but Dante beckons to Francesca and Paolo. She, the daughter of the ruler of Ravenna, had been married off to a son of the lord of Rimini, but fell in love with his other son Paolo who was already married. It was when they read of Lancelot's first embrace of Queen Guinevere that Paolo and Francesca could resist each other no longer: 'One day, to our delight, we read of Lancelot, how love constrained him ... When we read how that fond smile was kissed by such a lover, trembling he kissed my trembling mouth. We read no more that day.'

For transgressing the bonds of marriage, they were murdered by Francesca's outraged husband and damned, bound together for ever in the Inferno, doomed to continually try to repeat the adulterous kiss which was their downfall. Dante's medieval Christian God had a grim sense of humour.

The gods of the *Romaunt of the Rose* were much more apt to be forgiving. In the first part of the French allegorical poem, written by Guillaume de Lorris in about 1230, a Lover visits a mysterious garden. Idleness allows him to enter, and in the garden he finds Pleasure, Desire, Cupid and, among others, the Rose. Welcome gives him permission to kiss the Rose, but 4,000 verses later, after considering the issue from all angles, after discussing it with the likes of Hope, Fear,

Reason and Venus, the so-called Lover still has not decided whether or not to pluck the Rose. Shame, Scandal, Danger and Jealousy finally drive him away.

Forty years on, Jean de Meun added a cynical tone and 18,000 verses which treat the Rose, the allegorical lady of the *Romaunt of the Rose,* with the contempt that was usually bestowed on real women. The tone throughout is one of amused blasphemy, culminating in ironic prayers simultaneously to the pagan and Christian gods of love: 'With ardour I knelt between the two lovely pillars, consumed with a desire to worship the beautiful, sacred sanctuary with a devoted, a pious heart . . . I moved aside the curtain which covered the holy objects to explore the sacred place more intimately. I kissed the holy spot.'

Then he entered it, scattered some seed, and 'gave thanks, between delicious kisses, ten or twenty times to the god of Love, to Venus (who had helped me most) and to all the barons of the host (whose help I beg God grant to all true lovers).'

Just as in the fairy tale the prince would cut away thorns to arrive at the secret room in which lay Sleeping Beauty – Briar Rose was the Grimm brothers' name for her – so in this unsubtle antecedent, the Lover struggles to reach the holy Rose, and when he finds her, she just lies there and thinks of France.

THE PRINCE AND THE PROTOTYPE

Sleeping Beauty, I suspect, is Everyman's ideal woman: she who sleeps and waits. Utterly unmistakable in the earliest versions, the ideology of the fairy tale is that the girl is a *tabula rasa*, a blank sheet, on which the young man inscribes his fantasy. Because she is asleep, she gives him no trouble, no lip. He can do with her what he likes. In all the early tellings, he rapes her while she sleeps. Later, in the tales collected by the two Grimm brothers and in Disney, he awakens her with a kiss.

In the rambling, fourteenth-century, Arthurian prose romance, *Perceforest*, the prince was brutal, though we weren't to blame him for it. Princess Zellandine falls asleep the moment she starts to spin. When Prince Troylus comes upon the sleeping princess, there is nothing to stop him so he rapes her. She doesn't awaken.

In the *Pentamerone* – tales collected in the seventeenth century by a much-travelled Neapolitan – the story of Sleeping Beauty is very little changed: Talia, the daughter of a great lord, falls into a deep, enchanted sleep when she gets a splinter in her finger. The hero, already married, is a king out hunting in the forest who discovers the sleeping Talia and takes advantage of the situation: he 'plucked from her the fruits of love'. Talia becomes pregnant but doesn't wake until one of her babies accidentally sucks her finger instead of her breast – Freud would have told us it is no accident – and the splinter comes out.

In both these tales, Sleeping Beauty's real troubles begin when she wakes: evil jealous wives and evil jealous mothers make her and the prince's lives a misery.

The tale became sweeter when Charles Perrault moulded it into a children's story. The French civil servant's *The Sleeping Beauty in the Woods/La Belle au bois dormant* was the most influential early source of the fairy tale in English. Its first English-language edition was in 1729, three decades after its appearance in French. In this version, the enchanted sleep *begins* with a kiss. Seeing the princess fall asleep under the evil fairy's curse, her parents 'kissed their dear child without waking her' and departed to let the spell to take its course. Their kiss signifies their acceptance of their daughter's passive fate and puts the ball in the prince's court.

The rescuing Prince attacks thorns and briars to enter the castle but on arrival does nothing indelicate: 'At last, he came into a chamber all gilt with gold, where he saw upon a bed, the curtains of which were all open, the finest sight that ever was seen, a Princess ... He approached with trembling, and admiration, and fell down before her upon his knees.

'And now, as the enchantment was at an end, the princess awaked. Is it you my Prince, she said to him, you have waited a great while.'

There is a secret wedding in the palace in the woods, but only when his father dies, and he is crowned king, does the Prince openly acknowledge the children and Sleeping

Beauty. Then come her serious troubles with his mother, a cannibalistic ogress.

The first volume of *Nursery and Household Tales/ Kinder und Häus-marchen* by Jacob and Wilhelm Grimm appeared in Berlin in 1812, during the winter of Napoleon's retreat from Moscow. The Grimm brothers claimed to have come upon their versions independently from other known sources, culling their stories from old manuscripts and from local people who handed them down by word of mouth. The brothers' wives had an old nurse, *die alte Marie*, who had told them many traditional tales. The tale of Sleeping Beauty came direct, they said, from this old nurse.

In the Grimm brothers' story, when the prince entered the castle, 'He opened the door where Briar Rose lay. And when he saw her looking so lovely in her sleep, he could not turn away his eyes; and he stooped and kissed her, and she awaked, and opened her eyes and looked at him quite sweetly.' The whole castle wakes, the marriage is celebrated, there is no trouble with the in-laws, and they 'live contented to the end of their days'. This is the story that little girls have been taught to believe in; the romantic prototype.

In 1840, when it became the first of Planché's extravagant Covent Garden pantomimes, *Sleeping Beauty* had a sense of humour as well as a kiss:

Princess: Ah! was that you, my Prince, my lips who prest!'
Prince: She wakes! she speaks! and we shall still be blest!
    You're not offended?'
Princess: Oh, dear, not at all! Aren't you the gentleman
    who was to call?

Twenty years later, in *The Fairy Book* for children, the author Mrs Craik mentioned that the prince might have kissed the princess as she woke, 'but as nobody saw it, and she never told, we cannot be quite sure of the fact.' Most later story-tellers were certain, and made the kiss the cause of the awakening. In 1890, when the Tchaikovsky ballet *The Sleeping Beauty* opened in St Petersburg, Act 2, Scene 2 had Prince Florimund, already in love with the sleeper he has not seen, following the Lilac Fairy through the forest and the palace's cobwebs to Aurora, whom he awakens with a kiss.

In the perniciously charming C. S. Evans version, the newly kissed-awake princess is filled in on her own history by the prince:

> For the first time she heard the story of the enchantment, and her eyes grew round with wonder as she listened to her lover's account of the strange things that had happened in the castle. When he told of the great hedge and its cruel thorns, and of the many young men who died in trying to force their way through it, her eyes filled with tears.
>
> 'How great their courage was,' she sighed. 'Oh, if only I could bring them back to life.'
>
> But the Prince kissed her tears away and hastened past that part of his tale, and presently she was smiling again and happy, because she understood that everything had happened as it was bound to happen.

Oh dear. This is how it starts. And what it leads to is centuries of know-it-all lovers in literature and the movies. The more modern kisses awaken desire, but a heroine's chief virtues are still beauty and compliance. Many agree with the psychiatrist Bruno Bettelheim that Sleeping Beauty is about adolescent girls learning to accept their awakening sexuality. It seems to me more a lesson in accepting male sexuality being foisted upon the girl and the abnegation of her own: wait, and when he is ready, he will come. He must do what it takes to pursue his object; she has only to be that object.

To girls, it is a deadening lesson in passivity; to boys, a lesson in date rape.

The lesson is also that a curious young woman (who tries out spinning; work) will prick her finger and until she is rescued by her particular prince will remain lifeless, roleless – in suspended animation. It is the story of a girl who waits. He also has other quests. She has children.

Or, worse, she doesn't have children. Her only option then, even to modernists, is literal and psychological barrenness: 'What shall I do now? What shall I do?' is the plaintive refrain of the despairing woman in T. S. Eliot's poem *The Waste Land*. Naïve Sleeping Beauty slept through the torpor and the repressed dismay, and gave us false hopes of princes. But Eliot's woman, 'Pressing lidless eyes,' insomniac, is 'waiting for a knock upon the door', for the kiss of awakening to life which will never come. Eliot thought the twentieth century was in decline because the icons of faith had been smashed. The war was over and everyone was dead. Inside. He was not completely right, but it is certainly true that spiritless women inhabit a wasteland.

The fairy tale Sleeping Beauty, which today many people know only in its Walt Disney incarnation, is a tame corruption of the lascivious myths of Brynhild and Sigurd and Cupid and Psyche. Brynhild could fly, Psyche was eager and active; but in the fairy tale, she only serves who only sleeps and waits.

The kiss in Sleeping Beauty, a travesty of kissing, is the most unromantic kiss in the world. Comatose, she cannot possibly participate in it. The kiss, which is imposed on her, seals her supine fate.

But the story doesn't have to be like this. It wasn't always.

In an embryo of the tale, the ancient Norse *Volsunga Saga*, Brynhild – an active, opinionated, warrior goddess, a Valkyrie – is deprived of her divinity because she allowed herself to be surprised by a man. She and eight of her sisters, flying far from Valhalla, landed on earth, and took off their plumage. It was seized by King Agnar, putting the Valkyries under his power. Brynhild had no choice but to help him in the war he was fighting and to see that his enemy Hjalmgunnar was killed. Hjalmgunnar, though, was the protégé of her father Odin, the king of the gods. In aiding Odin's enemy, no matter what the circumstances, she was being disobedient to her father (also a sub-text of Sleeping Beauty, who has been forbidden to spin). As a goddess, Brynhild has had a lively life. Now, a woman, she must marry. Not just any prince will do. Such a heroine must have a suitably brave one. To make things appropriately difficult for prospective husbands, Brynhild is exiled to a rock ringed with fire. Knowing it might take a long time for the right hero to penetrate the ring, Brynhild's father pricks her finger with the thorn of sleep so that she will still be beautiful and young however long it takes.

The hero is Sigurd, Siegfried in Wagner's opera. He finds her through a self-kiss: his hands stained with the blood of a dragon he has killed, Sigurd puts his finger to his lips and is suddenly able to understand a bird singing its song of the sleeping Brynhild. Sigurd rushes off to find her, and conquers the flames. They kiss. He removes the armour from her body and gives her a ring. Then he leaves, and elsewhere after an enchanting evening (and an enchanted drink) he marries someone else. Instead of accepting her fate passively like Sleeping Beauty, Brynhild takes active revenge, arranging for Sigurd to be murdered. But she soon realizes that his death is not what she really wanted. In the hope of being with him in the next world, she throws herself onto his funeral pyre.

Not the best choice, granted, but at least she is the one making it.

Or take Shakespeare's Venus in her troubled affair with

Adonis. Like any self-respecting heroine she has *some* control of who kisses her when and where:

> Ile be a parke, and thou shalt be my deare:
> Feed where thou wilt, on mountaine, or in dale;
> Graze on my lips, and if those hils be drie,
> Stray lower, where the pleasant fountains lie.

Now that so few of us have a classical education, Venus's story, like that of Brynhild, is disappearing into the deepening mythological mists. So is the even better kiss story of Cupid and Psyche.

Medieval ballads and legends tell of fearless heroes daring to kiss dragons despite their hideous breath and profiles. But in the ancient myth of Cupid and Psyche, it is the princess who had to kiss the monster. In the earliest Orphic versions of the story, the monster Eros – later known as Cupid, the amorous god of love – was double-sexed and golden-winged; he had four heads, and like all lovers roared like a lion and hissed like a serpent or bleated like a lamb.

Psyche's father had been told by the oracle of Apollo to take her to a solitary mountain where she would be prey to a monster. The beautiful princess of whom Venus was jealous went to the mountain top expecting the worst. Like Sleeping Beauty and the character Beauty in the fairy tale *Beauty and the Beast*, Psyche (Soul in Greek) accommodatingly awaits her fate in a mysterious deserted palace. In the dark of night, a stranger who, she has been told, is an inhuman monster joins her. Cupid/Love comes to her only in the dark and will not reveal his identity to her (although he knows hers). Night after night, she enjoys his caresses but suffers a disquieting cognitive dissonance: 'although she loathed the animal she loved the husband it seemed to be.'

No decent soul can shut her eyes to reality for long. So

Psyche decides to take the initiative, to look. If she should see that she has been sharing her bed with a monster, no matter how good a lover, she will have no choice but to kill him.

In one hand she takes a knife, in the other a lighted lamp. In the flickering light she sees sleeping beside her the divinely handsome Cupid, his curly hair, golden and 'washed in ambrosia', straying prettily on to his flushed cheeks. At the foot of the bed are Cupid's bow and arrows, his 'gracious weapons' which she fondles, accidentally pricking her finger on one of the sharp arrows of love. Now she falls desperately in love with Love, and begins to kiss him everywhere, with deep, passionate, open-mouthed, kisses, hoping he will not wake. She too for the moment wants a sleeping beauty.

But either from envy or ardour, the lamp spurts its hot oil on to Cupid, who wakes. Psyche becomes even more ardent, but all the beseeching kisses in the world cannot stop him fleeing: Cupid spread his wings and flew away from the kisses and embraces of Pysche without a word; but not before she had seized his right leg with both hands and clinging to it, was carried up through the cloudy sky; but soon her strength failed her and she tumbled down to earth.

Psyche forgave him, though not everyone would. Cupid's flight from her kisses has been interpreted both as a symbolic demand for a maturer love and as a lesson that things aren't always perfect the first time. It has been seen as a suggestion to the soul that it take an alternative path, the Platonic one. It has been read, too, as the often unhappy fate of the assertive woman. Cupid's insistence on the darkness also, they say, tells us that Love–Eros cannot be understood by reason.

I think Cupid's flight was sheer panic: a reflex response to the physical pain of hot oil and the psychological one of exposure.

Not many people know the rest of the story, which is that

Psyche, a valiant soul, didn't give up and got him back. By undertaking a series of herculean tasks, and accomplishing them just like any other Greek hero, Psyche attained her object. As a reward for her long and arduous labours, she was made immortal and moved up to Olympus with Cupid, who regretted his flight, and there they lived ever after.

Yet the stories that continue in the repertory, the ones that are told over and over to a wide audience, are of a virgin being kissed while she sleeps, or of girls forced for reasons beyond their control to kiss ugly male beasts. In the nineteenth century, folklorists had already found stories in seven European or Asian languages in which a virginal young woman was wedded to a bear, a goat, a monkey or a wolf, not to mention a stove, all of which are transformed into men. In an African version, it is a crocodile. These stories with animal bridegrooms, of which *The Frog Prince* and *Beauty and the Beast* are just the most famous, hold out the hope, Marina Warner says, that although her father has placed the princess in the care of a monster, he'll change into a perfect prince. The truth, of course, is that it is the young woman who must change, who must find something to love in him. The story is good social training, providing the lie she must tell herself to accomplish this.

In Madame de Villeneuve's eighteenth-century *Beauty and the Beast,* it soon becomes apparent we have a female author at work: 'How many girls', Beauty wonders, 'are compelled to marry rich brutes – much more brutish than the Beast, who's only one in form and not in his feelings or his actions.' In an earlier tale with a similar twist, Madame d'Aulnoy has her heroine Hidessa in bed in the dark with someone, and perfectly happy too until she turns on the light. Her bed partner turns out to be the ugly Green Serpent. He vanishes; her lessons in compliance, which now begin in earnest, include three years of isolation after which even a serpent's hiss sounds inviting. Accepted entirely on his terms – warts, hisses and all – he turns into a handsome prince. In some versions she kisses him, in others not. The sub-text of the tale seems to be that sexuality will turn out to be the serpent/prince's saving grace, one lesson to the budding bride being the old saw that everyone looks the same in the dark.

The princess accepts the frog or the beast, and he is transformed into a prince – often at the moment she kisses him. Yet these tales are read not as the story of the frozen sexuality of the prince, but as the story of Beauty growing up.

In the early nineteenth century, when Sir Walter Scott read the Grimm brothers' tale *The Frog King*, now known as *The Frog Prince*, it reminded him of a story from his childhood, the legend of Prince Paddock, in which a princess sent to get water at the Well of the World's End is helped by a frog and lightly promises to become its bride. It turns out she must. In some versions, the frog threatens the girl: unless she marries him, she will be torn to pieces. In all versions, the frog is pushy, and the princess naïve. She makes a disadvantageous deal with the frog which the powers that be (usually her father) insist she hold to. In the Grimm version, the princess's ball falls into a pond and the frog offers to recover it if she will allow him to be her companion, eating from her plate, sleeping in her bed. Thinking no frog can do that anyway, she agrees. But the frog insists. Instead of throwing him out of the castle – after all, the older frog has taken advantage of her inexperience in making the bargain – her father makes her stick to its terms. The more the princess tries to withstand the frog's unreasonable demands, the more the king her father insists that she must keep her promise to the full.

We have discussed what this teaches the girl. What it teaches little boys, who will identify with the frog, is that when a girl says no she really means yes. The princess must give in and accede to the demands of her father, who is the king, and the demands of the frog, who will be revealed to be a king. In the Grimms' version, the princess throws the frog against the wall, and still can't get rid of him; he turns into a prince, and 'He by her father's will was now her dear companion and husband.'

The frog, we are told by psychoanalysts, is a penis. She will like it in the end. The bottom line is that either a young woman who is absurdly dutiful, as in *Beauty and the Beast,* or a child who has been tricked by an older frog must learn to accept a monster as her bridegroom. What was in Cupid and Psyche a passionate tale of lust and daring has become a prim one of socialization.

Unfortunately, from the Palace's point of view, Princess Diana did not turn out to be a passive and compliant Sleeping Beauty. Unforgivably, from every romantic's point of view, the Prince has now admitted with his own lips that he never truly loved her; his father insisted he marry her. Was their kiss on the balcony of Buckingham Palace after the wedding – a kiss which seemed to be the very incarnation of story-book romance – mere pageantry? Was it form instead of content? Pomp instead of passion? Was it a hoax? Television cameras trained on the Palace merely recorded the totality, the iconic kiss. It was left to us to decipher it. What did the kiss mean?

The act of meaning something, so the latest thinking goes, is interpersonal. Like all communication it is a co-operative act.

This particular wedding kiss, more than most, became a rite linking the public and the private. It communicated the couple's new status to each other and to the rest of us in a cultural code we understand. Via television it linked the global village. It also linked the diminished political present of Britain to the royal splendour of its past. The kiss was simultaneously an advertisement for the monarchy (and for Monarchy) and an invitation to the fairyland world of glass coaches and enchantment.

And even if he never loved her – fie! – he was for a time, said those close to the Prince, sexually enthralled by her. Infatuated. And she by him. If it was not true love we saw in the kiss, it was honest lust.

What was phoney was the story we told ourselves, our perception of romance. The kiss told us, we pretended, that the fairy tale still worked. That virgins still existed and their reward was princes. That love could conquer all – the compatibility gap, the generation gap, even the fact that the new princess had not been asleep for a hundred years and that perhaps the prince had.

Soon after she kissed him, Prince Charming turned into a Frog: unfaithful, unloving, ungallant. The Princess woke up and stood up for herself, breaking the spell. Has she shattered at last the myth of Sleeping Beauty?

BODY AND SOUL

Newly-weds who had difficulty consummating their marriage used to blame the trouble on a bad spell having been cast; in seventeenth-century France, it could be countered by kissing in a prescribed manner. Both partners had to be active to break the spell, and completely nude. The husband began by kissing the wife's big toe on the left foot, the wife by kissing her husband's big toe. Perhaps this did not so much break the evil spell as begin to cast a new one.

It is, though, the union of souls, not bodies, that wedding kisses traditionally signify. Breath, the life force, was thought to contain the soul. In the mouth-to-mouth kiss the two lovers were exchanging the breath of life, mingling their souls. Christopher Marlowe's Dr Faustus believed it, yet sold his soul to the devil:

> Sweet Helen, make me immortal with a kiss!
> Her lips suck forth my soul: see where it flies!

At a marriage Mass a twelfth-century bridegroom went to the altar to receive the *pax* from the priest, returned to his bride, and gave her the *pax* by kissing her. If, after the *osculum interveniens*, one partner died, the wedding gifts did not have to not be returned. Their souls were as one. This idea of merging souls would run and run. 'Soul meets soul on lover's lips,' Shelley wrote in the nineteenth century.

The soul-mingling kiss, which could do double duty as an emblem of religious or sexual ecstasy, gave erotic love an acceptable Christian face. The notion of a kiss touching the soul was, however, an old one: 'My soul was on my lips as I was kissing Agathon,' wrote Plato.

The Renaissance poet Robert Herrick absorbs the idea and states it matter-of-factly in 'Love Palpable', one of his lesser lyrics:

> I prest my Julia's lips, and in the kisse,
> Her Soule and Love were palpable in this.

Among classically educated gentlemen the notion was so commonplace that the seventeenth-century poet John Donne could allude to it lightly in a letter: 'Sir, more than kisses, letters mingle souls.'

The super-sophisticate Alexander Pope wrote the poem *Eloisa to Abelard* (1717) about the disgraced medieval lovers Heloïse and Abelard. After she became a nun, you may remember, Heloïse suggested that castration might cure Abelard, but nothing would abate her own desire. In Pope's poem Eloisa wants to die kissing Abelard:

> Thou, Abelard! the last sad office pay,
> And smooth my passage to the realms of day;
> See my lips tremble and my eyeballs roll,
> Suck my last breath, and catch my flying soul!

In Goethe's *Werther* (1774), Werther and Charlotte kissed fatally after reading Ossian. A quarter of a century later, the mesmeric power of literature was demonstrated again when, after a discussion of Petrarch's love poetry and a recital of Sappho's poems, the Italian writer Foscolo's Jacopo and Teresa felt they had no option but to kiss. Dante's Paolo and Francesca had also succumbed to temptation after reading about a kiss. Jacopo eroticizes his death by thinking with his last thoughts about the kiss which joined his and Teresa's souls: 'And our lips and our breaths were intermingled, and my soul was transfused into your breast.'

To die with your lover's kiss on your lips was an ideal of both medieval romance and melodramatic nineteenth-century poetry. Shelley the radical believed, as Dante had, in the soul-mingling kiss, and in 'Epipsychidion' almost makes us believe in the possibility:

> And our veins beat together; and our lips
> With other eloquence than words, eclipse
> The soul that burns between them,
> . . .
> As mountain-springs under the morning Sun.
> We shall become the same, we shall be one
> Spirit within two frames.

To hear Shelley tell it in 'Love's Philosophy', everything kisses:

> See the mountains kiss high Heaven,
> . . .
> And the moonbeams kiss the sea:
> What are all these kissings worth
> If thou kiss not me?

117

Emily Dickinson spoke of Nature kissing too, but in her poems, people didn't. That eloquent blasphemer Sara Teasdale, who wrote in the first decade of the twentieth century, goes further:

> Before you kissed me only the wind of heaven
> Had kissed me and the tenderness of rain –
> Now you have come, how can I care for kisses
> Like theirs again?
>
> I sought the sea, she sent her winds to meet me,
> They surged about me singing of the south –
> I turned away to keep still holy
> Your kiss upon my mouth.

In *Diary of the Seducer* the Danish philosopher Kierkegaard uses the same imagery in chronicling the growing ardour of the woman he wants: 'She kisses me as dispassionately as heaven kisses the sea, softly and quietly as the dew kisses a flower, solemnly as the sea kisses the image of the moon.' A century later, in *London Fields,* the British novelist Martin Amis would translate the much over-used kiss-of-dew metaphor into comedy: 'As I walked under a tree, I felt the warm kiss of a voluptuous dewdrop on my crown. Gratefully I ran a hand through my hair and what do I find? Birdshit. Pigeonshit.'

That notoriously prudish Victorian Henry James, however, took the relationship of the kiss to the forces of nature seriously. In the first edition of his novel *Portrait of a Lady*, 'His kiss was like a flash of lightning; when it was dark again she was free.' In the later, definitive edition of the novel, the kiss was more firmly imagined: 'His kiss was like white lightning, a flash that spread, and spread again, and stayed; and it was extraordinary, as if, while she took it she felt each thing in his hard manhood that had least pleased her, each aggressive fact of his face, his figure, his presence, justified of its intense identity and made one with this act of possession. So had she heard of those wrecked and under water following a train of images before they sink. But when darkness returned she was free.'

In the secularized world, kisses didn't unite us in death, they united or shackled us in life. In Scott Fitzgerald's novel of the 1920s, *The Great Gatsby*, one can see the continuing tradition of souls commingling. Enthralled by Daisy, Gatsby really doesn't hesitate even though he sees the kiss as dangerous; it will force him, he believes, to live in the social world, placed. It will be the end of all of his grandiose plans except for that of social climbing:

> His heart beat faster and faster as Daisy's white face came up to his own. He knew that when he kissed this girl, and forever wed his unutterable visions to her perishable breath, his mind would never romp again like the mind of God. So he waited, listening for a moment longer to the tuning-fork that had been struck upon a star. Then he kissed her. At his lips' touch she blossomed for him like a flower and the incarnation was complete.

It is, though, an illusion. Daisy is less than she seems; Gatsby does not find happiness.

Virginia Woolf's heroine in *Mrs Dalloway* is equally deluded. On the day in which the novel begins and ends, the rich and fashionable Clarissa Dalloway, wife of a prominent Member of Parliament, walks through London, thinking of this and that. In her stream of consciousness, we glimpse the kiss that the heroine believes to be the defining moment of her life: She and Sally fell a little behind the others:

119

Then came the most exquisite moment of her whole life passing a stone urn with flowers in it. Sally stopped; picked a flower; kissed her on the lips.

. . . she felt that she had been given a present, wrapped up, and told just to keep it, not to look at it – a diamond, something infinitely precious, wrapped up, which, as they walked (up and down, up and down), she uncovered, or the radiance burnt through, the revelation, the religious feeling!

The first kiss that transforms one's life sounds terribly old-fashioned, but it continues to crop up in contemporary novels. In *Leviathan*, Paul Auster's hero must first withstand a distasteful kiss of adultery. When his best friend's wife Fanny expresses interest – 'You don't have to tie yourself up in knots. If you want me, you can have me,' – the hero is dismayed. 'I found her assertiveness daunting, incomprehensible.' The kiss inflicted upon him is hideous: 'She stood up from her chair and walked around the table to where I was sitting. I opened my arms to her, and without saying a word she crawled into my lap, planted her haunches firmly against my thighs, and took hold of my face with her hands. We started kissing. Mouths open, tongues thrashing, slobbering onto each other's chins.'

The Austerian adulterous kiss is ugly and physical; true love is beautiful and bodiless, the zipless fuck becoming the tongueless kiss. When the protagonist encounters true love, not only does the woman in question have a much more innocent name – Iris; she belongs to no one else, indeed she scarcely knows the host. She comes with no label, a blank computer screen on which to enter his fantasy. Within seconds of their meeting, our hero begins to construct his myth and drag her into it. He takes out his wallet and shows her snapshots of his little son.

To listen to Iris recall that evening now, it was at that moment that she decided she was in love with me, that she understood I was the person she was going to marry. It took me a little longer to understand how I felt about her, but only by a few hours.

They left the party together, had dinner at a restaurant, drinks elsewhere, and then, before midnight, he hails her a taxi:

but before I opened the door to let her in, I reached out and grabbed her, drawing her close to me and kissing her deep inside the mouth. It was one of the most impetuous things I have ever done, a moment of insane, unbridled passion. The cab drove off, and Iris and I continued standing in the middle of the street, wrapped in each other's arms. It was as though we were the first people who had ever kissed, as though we invented the art of kissing together that night. By the next morning, Iris had become my happy ending.

Like Henry James's bolt of lightning, this first kiss ends with an allusion to the elements: 'We took each other by storm, and nothing has ever been the same for me since.'

In the twentieth century, one's *very* first kiss is more often not about lust or love, infatuation or intimacy. It is an unsensual rite of passage, an unromantic jolt into what one hopes will be adulthood. No one had more such first kisses than Mickey Rooney and Judy Garland in their string of movie comedies that bridged the thirties and the forties. In their last encounter, in *Girl Crazy,* Rooney asks Garland, 'Did I ever tell you that a fella in my state of mind is apt to kiss a girl in your state of mind?'

'I dare you,' she replies. 'I double dare you.'

The kiss, when it happens, is all pucker. These two know where the noses go, but not the tongues. They don't even know kissing involves tongues. (If they went to the movies nowadays, they would find that out.) To them, pressing lip to lip means a joining in maturity. It is just another version of that children's kissing game, spin the bottle. Their kiss is like taking your first cigarette.

The Rooney–Garland kisses weren't stand-ins for orgasm or intimacy. They were kisses of affection, to be sure; but, above all in this early series of teen films, they were ritual kisses, Hollywood's sexual equivalent of the graduation or bar mitzvah kiss.

That other children's game, skipping, was once associated with spring planting. It was thought, it is hard to know just how seriously, that crops would grow only as high as those performing the ritual could jump. As you jumped, seeds buried underground would spring into life. One traditional skipping chant goes:

> Butterfly, butterfly, kiss, kiss, kiss
> Jump out before you miss, miss, miss

Bulfinch, the nineteenth century's favourite mythographer, explains that the Greek word *psyche* meant 'butterfly' as well as 'soul': 'There is no illustration of the immortality of the soul so striking and beautiful as the butterfly, bursting on brilliant wings from the tomb in which it has lain, after a dull, grovelling, caterpillar existence, to flutter in the blaze of day and feed on the most fragrant and delicate productions of the spring.' In the myth of Cupid and Psyche, he says, 'Psyche, then, is the human soul, which is purified by sufferings and misfortunes and is thus prepared for the enjoyment of true and pure happiness.' In death, not life.

This idea led to the use of Cupid and Psyche as decorations

on tombs. Well-to-do pagans in ancient Rome had copies made of the fourth-century BC Capitoline sculpture in which Cupid (the god of love) kisses Psyche (the soul), instilling eternal bliss. Cleverly, the early Christians used the same imagery on their tombs; choosing an image that was already popular did not attract unwanted attention. All they had to do was reinterpret it so that the god of love kisses the Christian's soul to bestow eternal life. It is just possible to see how over the centuries, in a kind of Chinese whispers, a religious idea of the Sleeping Beauty – that of the dead soul awaiting the kiss of eternity – might have arisen. This got an erotic spin in her awakening to the erotic life.

Shakespeare handles the whole issue of teen romance much more deftly in *Romeo and Juliet*, titillating us by mingling the religious and the erotic:

Romeo: Have not saints lips, and holy palmers too?
Juliet: Ay, pilgrim, lips that they must use in prayer.

However, Romeo uses his lips in kissing instead of prayer. In their dialogue, the word sin becomes code for kiss.

Romeo: Then move not, while my prayers effect I take.
            (*He kisses her.*)
            Thus from my lips, by yours, my sin is purged.
Juliet: Then have my lips the sin that they have took.
Romeo: Sin from my lips? O trespass sweetly urged!
            Give me my sin again. (*He kisses her.*)

Despite the ecstatic mutual blasphemy, the opposition of their warring families overwhelms them; at the end of Shakespeare's first romantic tragedy the two thirteen-year-olds lie dead.

A kiss between a mature black woman and a middle-aged

Hasidic Jewish man caused a furore when it appeared on the cover of *The New Yorker* for Valentine's Day 1993 at a time when blacks and Jews were at war in Brooklyn. No one mentioned Romeo and Juliet, but many thought of *West Side Story*, with its New Yorkers from warring clans: Tony, who is Irish, and Maria, Puerto Rican. The modern Romeo, Tony, sings ecstatically that he has just kissed a girl named Maria.

All ends less than well, too, for the star-crossed lovers in Vikram Seth's *A Suitable Boy*:

> They sat on the twisted root of the twin banyan trees. Lata was at a loss as to what to say. She heard herself saying:
>
> 'Kabir, are you interested in politics?'
>
> He looked at her in amazement at the unexpected question, then simply said, 'No,' and kissed her.
>
> Her heart turned over completely. She responded to his kiss – without thinking anything out – but with a sense of amazement at herself – that she should be so reckless and happy.
>
> When the kiss was over, Lata suddenly began thinking again, and more furiously than ever.
>
> 'I love you,' said Kabir.
>
> When she was silent, he said:
>
> 'Well, aren't you going to say anything?'
>
> 'Oh, I love you too,' said Lata, stating a fact that was completely obvious to her and therefore should have been obvious to him. 'But it's pointless.'

Instead of betrothal, their kiss leads to a discussion of religious difference. He is Muslim; she Hindu. The Montagues and the Capulets.

When he was about to cycle off, she said to him:

'Have you kissed anyone else?'

'What was that?' He looked amused.

She was looking at his face. She didn't repeat the question . . .

'Do you mean ever?' he asked. 'No. I don't think so. Not seriously.'

And he rode off.

Unlike Juliet, Lata respects her family's wishes; and she is fearful of passion taking her over. She will choose to marry someone else. Partly because it reveals the strength of her own feelings to Lata, this promising first kiss becomes the kiss of death to her and Kabir's joint future.

The kiss of death is more literal, more lethal too, when one of the devil's advocates – a mafioso or a vampire – bestows it. The vampire's kiss is the reverse of the traditional soul-touching kiss. Instead of feeding the 'soul', the kiss of the vampire sucks away life, allows evil to penetrate and destroys moral fibre. *Dracula*, which appeared at the turn of the nineteenth century, was not the first vampire story, but it was the first to impose itself on the popular imagination. The reek of unpleasant sexuality in Bram Stoker's *fin de siècle* novel of decadence was not unintentional. A hundred years later, *Dracula* continues to inspire movies, plays and novels about the Count from Transylvania and other depraved vampires, often with darkly sexual implications.

VAMPIRES AND OTHER FATAL ATTRACTIONS

More than most people, the playwright and poet Oscar Wilde doubted the importance of being earnest; but he was in 'The Ballad of Reading Gaol', where he wrote about the affair that ruined his life:

> And all men kill the thing they love,
> By all let this be heard,
> Some do it with a bitter look,
> Some with a flattering word,
> The coward does it with a kiss,
> The brave man with a sword!

The love affair with Bosie, Lord Alfred Douglas, led to Wilde's destruction, not to Bosie's. Younger but no innocent, the urbane Bosie was the son of the Marquess of Queensberry. When the disapproving marquess publicly insulted Wilde, he sued for libel. This started a chain of events which led to the trial in 1895 at which Oscar Wilde was found guilty of homosexual offences and sentenced to two years' hard labour.

Two years after the trial *Dracula* appeared.

To see Wilde in Count Dracula requires arduous squinting, but many commentators have made the vicious equation of vampirism and homosexuality. The sensationalized Wilde trial aroused a conservative moral backlash which Bram Stoker's novel certainly did nothing to restrain and quite possibly fuelled. Written at a time when sex could kill with syphilis, *Dracula* has spawned a spate of imitations in an era when sex can kill with AIDS.

Symbolically, a vampire's kiss signifies moral death. It steals the soul and the peace of heavenly rest. One either dies outright or joins the legions of the undead preying on the living, destroying decency. Much of the power of vampire imagery lies in its inversion of the more usual meanings of a kiss. Like a black mass, the kiss of the vampire is an inversion of the good. In the climate in which *Dracula* was written, homophobia was inherent in the imagery. At one time, homosexuals were called 'inverts'; Radcliffe Hall uses the term for lesbians in her 1920s novel *The Well of Loneliness*.

Like the kiss of Judas, the vampire's kiss of death is a betrayal. Stoker himself equates Dracula with Judas: 'In silence we returned to the library, and after a minute or two I went to my own rooms. The last I saw of Count Dracula was his kissing his hand to me, with a red light of triumph in his eyes, and with a smile that Judas in hell might be proud of.'

Count Dracula particularly likes transforming pretty women into vampires; and they, like any medieval witch-to-be, are usually too weak-minded to resist. To potential male victims, Dracula's minions are alluring: 'All three had brilliant white teeth, that shone like pearls against the ruby of their voluptuous lips . . . I felt in my heart a wicked burning desire that they would kiss me with those red lips.' But of course their kisses kill or contaminate: 'Friend Arthur, if you had met that kiss . . . you would in time, when you had died, have become *nosferatu*, as they call it in Eastern Europe, [one of] those Undeads that so have filled us with horror.' Instead of embodying mutual nurturance, intimacy, love, the vampire's kiss is selfish and deadly. It partakes of an inverse alchemy, transmuting the loving kiss, which were it a precious metal would be gold, into morally poisonous lead.

Nosferatu, the first movie version of *Dracula*, an eerie German Expressionist film made in 1922, got the vampiric mouth and therefore the kiss right. Hideous, with the mouth of a rodent, batlike ears, and horrible spidery fingers, *Nosferatu*'s vampire has been called a phallus with teeth. To bestow his penetrative vampire's kiss, he pinched the skin between his fangs, two incisors on the upper gum, two on the lower. In more modern versions the vampire usually has just two upper fangs with which he punctures the aorta. *Nosferatu*'s bite is less dramatic but more efficient. This film makes the connection of sex, disease and death vivid when rats pour off a ship and the plague arrives in the town.

The novel *Interview with the Vampire* by Anne Rice is told through the eyes of Louis, a sensitive man who, having lost those close to him, wishes for his own death. The vampire Lestat delivers it after a fashion. In the movie version he appears one evening in Louis' life, bites his neck, drinks Louis' blood right up to the point of death, and then gives him a choice – he *can* die, or he can drink blood from Lestat, which will at once revitalize him and transform him into a vampire. Louis drinks. There is an intense exchange – more like a kiss than a mere feeding. The two enact a vampiric intercourse. Heartbeats quicken, blood rises, Louis tremors. He has been blooded.

Lestat makes the orphan Claudia into a vampire so that Louis will have a companion and stop moping. The child vampire brings Lestat his favourite evening treat – two young, plump, warm-blooded boys who are dead but seem only to be asleep. When Lestat sucks the dead blood of the boys, he is weakened as though by poison and Claudia is able to cut off his head and incinerate him. Not much is made of the prospect of contaminated blood in this scene, in the film it is never again mentioned; but burning is how one safely disposes of victims of contagions like plague. Lestat survives. We next see him making another convert to vampirism in contemporary San Francisco, a city famous for its gay population. Like Coppola's movie *Dracula* and the recent spate of vampire novels, this film is trying hard to make a statement about AIDS.

Interestingly, vampire bats, small creatures which sometimes attack humans but prey mainly on cattle and sheep, kill not by draining their victim's blood, the amount lost being fairly minimal, but by transmitting diseases with their razor-sharp teeth. By bringing death, the fictional human vampire's kiss repudiates what we have been told by scientists: that kissing is unlikely to transmit AIDS. Both syphilis and AIDS are transmitted by bodily fluids; unlikely with any kiss, except that of the vampire in which the lips and the tongue are supplanted by fangs.

Much more realistic is the scene in *The Day of the Jackal* where the hero pinches the carotid of the woman he is kissing, transforming a kiss of passion into a kiss of death.

The kiss of the vampire breaks the skin of the neck, enters an artery, and so subverts the mutual feasting of the kiss; one partner has a solitary feast. In Rice's novel, the line between kissing and biting, sucking, feeding is blurry, but in the film *Interview with the Vampire* there is much less ambiguity with regard to the vampires' oral behaviour. There is plenty of biting, feeding, sucking but little kissing – no nuzzling – no actual osculation on the screen. Instead, there is the quintessential kiss of the vampire. As in the prototype *Dracula*, the moment a willing virgin expects the ecstasy of his lips on hers, the fangs come out, he veers from the mouth and *penetrates* her neck.

How much less dangerous is telephone sex, in which the soul as well as the body is untouched.

'And do you have one of those legendary Water Pik shower-massage heads?' asks the caller in the novelist Nicholson Baker's version of contemporary anti-intimacy *Vox*:

> 'I do, but I don't use it with any of the special settings. It was installed already when I moved in. It's useful for cleaning the tub. But when I'm – I don't hold it or put it between my legs or anything. I just treat it as a regular showerhead. What I do is . . .'
>
> 'Yes?'
>
> 'When I start to come?'
>
> 'Yes?'
>
> 'I—'
>
> 'Yes?'
>
> 'I open my mouth and let it fill with water. The feeling of the water overflowing my mouth . . . You there?'
>
> '*Don't* stop talking.'

Nicholson Baker's onanistic *femme fatale* is much less interesting than her literary and cinematic ancestor, the vamp. A moral if not a literal vampire, this stock character predates Stoker's novel.

Well before the turn of the nineteenth century, certain writers had become notorious for their depictions of sexual dominatrices to whom men submitted eagerly and with ecstasy. It was after reading *Venus in Furs* (1870) by Leopold von Sacher-Masoch, an Austrian with a day job as a lawyer, that the psychiatrist Krafft-Ebing invented the word 'masochism'. In the passage that follows, the hero Gregor, having allowed himself to be tied to a massive pillar that supports the oversized bed, submits to the lashes of Wanda's whip:

> With wild grace she rolled up her fur-lined sleeve and struck me across the back . . . the whip cut like a knife into my flesh . . . I gritted my teeth to avoid screaming. She struck me in the face, warm blood trickled down my brow but she laughed . . . 'What joy to have someone so completely in my power, and a man at that . . . I'll tear you to pieces, and with each lash of the whip my pleasure will grow. Now, twist like a worm, scream, whine.'

Finally she tires, tosses the whip aside, stretches out on an ottoman, and has him cut down:

> I approached the beautiful woman. Never did she seem more seductive to me than today with all her cruelty and contempt.
>
> 'One step further,' Wanda commanded. 'Now kneel down, and kiss my foot.'
>
> She extended her foot from beneath the hem of white satin, and I, a suprasensual fool, pressed my lips upon it.

Not even the hand that beat him, merely her foot is offered; the kiss furthers his abasement.

In *Afternoon Song*, the French poet Charles Baudelaire, who thought of women as tigresses and knew them to be deadly – he was wracked with syphilis – more literally expressed the idea of a woman whose love inflicted hurt:

On Kissing

> Sometimes, seeking to rage
> Your mysterious dark rage,
> Pecking pain into my bliss,
> You will bite me as you kiss

In the long narrative poem *Dolores* (1866), the British poet Algernon Swinburne revelled in pain:

> Though the kisses are bloody,
> Though they sting till it shudder and smart.

The poem, which beseeches Our Lady of Pain for physical abuse, evoked verbal abuse from the critics. The polite ones called Swinburne decadent.

> By the ravenous teeth that have smitten,
> Through kisses that blossom and bud,
> By the lips intertwisted and bitten,
> Till the foam has a savour of blood,
> By the pulse as it rises and falters,
> By the hands as they slacken and strain,
> *I* adjure thee, respond from thy altars,
> Our Lady of Pain.

He seeks ever new pleasures in the pain:

> From the lips and the foam and the fangs
> Shall no new sin be born for men's trouble,
> No dream of impossible pangs?

The painter Philip Burne-Jones made the next decisive move in the development of the vamp. Inspired by the success of *Dracula*, Burne-Jones gave the tradition of *La Belle Dame sans Merci* a bloodthirsty spin. A decade after *Dracula* had etched the vampire on the cultural map, Burne-Jones exhibited his picture *The Vampire* in the 1907 summer show at the New Gallery in London. In the painting, a wraith-like, carnivorous-looking woman is poised over a male corpse, her teeth marks visible on his skin. The unwholesome eroticism of the painting appealed to the late Victorian mind.

Rudyard Kipling, a relative of Burne-Jones, was inspired to write a rather bad poem about a man in love with a vamp: 'A fool there was and he made his prayer,' to 'the woman who did not care'. Forty years after Sacher-Masoch's hero had called himself a suprasensual fool, the idea was new again. The hit Broadway play of 1909 was *A Fool There Was,* a spin-off from Kipling's poem which featured a sexually predatory woman. The movie rights were bought by the mogul William Fox, but before the movie could be produced another studio jumped in and made *The Vampire* (1913), in which a man leaves his wholesome country life and wholesome sweetheart to seek opportunity in the city. There he meets a vampiric, a bad woman, who as he lies helpless on the ground dances for joy at the visible signs of his destruction.

A year later came the movie version of *A Fool There Was.* It was Theodosia Goodman's first film. It and she, under her stage name Theda Bara, immediately became bankable and the movie vamp was born. Short for vampire, the term vamp soon became American for *femme fatale*. In *A Fool There Was* she seduces a promising diplomat who is en route to a posting in Europe. With his career, his finances and his marriage sucked dry, the morally desiccated hero is deserted by Bara the vamp. Just as his saintly wife is about to take the undeserving man back, the vamp returns and commands, 'Kiss me, my fool!' He falls into her arms, a doomed man, evil conquering all.

With so many women of the period out of reach on the pedestal, the vamp's aggressive sexuality was particularly titillating. It was a time, too, when nice girls were becoming bold politically, and that worried some. The film historian Herbert Reynolds argues that the eager transformation of the legendary male vampire into the female vamp early in the century was a 'response to the surge in feminism (demonstrably in the demand for universal suffrage)'. Many people were scared that the independent woman of the future would be a man-eater. The movies fed that fear and in the scare figure of vamp played it for all it was worth. Theda Bara would play history's renowned vamps including Salome, Madame DuBarry and Cleopatra. The female whose kisses could kill morally would become an increasingly menacing fatal attraction. The vamp was deadlier than the male. The vampire genre film was minor; vamps, however, took centre stage. Glenn Close's role in *Fatal Attraction* (1987) is no more than a modern version of the sado-masochistic myth of vamp; the independent woman who is deadly. The roster of the *femme fatale* would include, not least of all, Garbo.

Garbo's icy beauty could raise the temperature of an international audience, and in *Flesh and the Devil* (1927), her kisses with John Gilbert were thought to be at the very edge of propriety. Gilbert was Valentino's successor as the great lover of the silent screen, and it was widely rumoured that he was Garbo's real-life lover. This added to the titillation. It is said that the director and cameramen tiptoed off the set of *Flesh and the Devil* because the stars were continuing the kiss scene undirected. Today the kisses of Gilbert seem oddly chaste. But not hers.

She plays a married woman having an illicit affair: 'My only excuse is I love you,' Garbo tells Gilbert. He, an officer, is expected to be a gentleman, not an adulterer, but is irresistibly drawn to her when he first sees her at the train station. Seeing her again across a crowded ballroom, he asks her to dance, and when she rises to do so, Garbo approaches him lips first. As they dance the proximity of their lips is an implied kiss. Very soon she leads him out of the ballroom and down the deserted garden path, where she sits on a bench in a secluded spot.

Smitten and astonished at her boldness, he sits down beside her, but he is the fly in the trap, not the spider. 'Who are you?' he asks.

'What does it matter?' She asks for a cigarette, an erstwhile sexual symbol which has lost its allure. *She* puts the cigarette in his mouth to light. In the light of the match we see their faces close, she leaning in to him. She blows out the match.

'You know . . . when you blow out the match,' he says, 'that's an invitation to kiss you.' As she doesn't reply, he accepts the invitation. The kiss is shot in close up, we see heads and part of a shoulder, the camera's close focus builds the intensity, the strong horizontal is hers, her arm pulling round his neck. She is the aggressor; the woman who does not wait.

The famous kiss of this movie is typically Garbo in that it is active and horizontal: she is lying on a divan, her head on a pillow; he bends over her and presses his lips to her cheek. Her hand at the nape of his neck, beneath the open collar of his uniform, pulls him closer; her lips are parted. Chaste though this kiss is, it conveys passion. Then their positions reverse. He reclines against the divan and she sits up and, from above, lingeringly kisses him on the lips. Again she uses her hand, one of the signatures of the Garbo kiss, holding the back of his head in place. Here, his is the upturned neck that would become so characteristic of the female kissee in future movies.

In *Mata Hari*, remember, her kiss extinguished the Madonna's lamp and destroyed all that is holy. The film-goer already understood the convention that whenever a woman was forward something unnatural and bad must be present. Here is the seed of *Fatal Attraction*.

What it sprouts into is the at first funny, then nasty personal *Kama Sutra* which the novelist Martin Amis constructs for his *London Fields* anti-heroine Nicola Six, whose 'tongue was long and powerful and as sharp-pronged as a sting. That mouth was a deep source, a deep source of lies and kisses.' The omniscient narrator, it would appear, is bitter. The vamp Nicola's kisses may be tight-lipped and pseudo-virginal, or 'as searching and detailed as a peridontal review: you came out from under them entirely plaque-free. The Rosebud, the Dry Application, Anybody's, Clash of the Incisors . . .' The list continues. For no apparent reason, what is billed as Nicola's most mercenary and manipulative manoeuvre is called the Jewish Princess kiss:

> Rich, vulgar, young, plump . . . the Jewish Princess was *all* tongue – and not its tip but its trunk, its meat: brute tongue. Here, the tongue did duty for every organ, male and female, the heart included. [The kiss was] more a weapon than a wand . . . it was almost unusably powerful. The Jewish Princess was *inordinate*. Applied at the right moment, it made a man kneel on the floor with his chequebook in his hands . . .
>
> The kiss was called the Jewish Princess – unforgivably. But then the kiss itself was unforgivable. The Jewish Princess was unforgivable.

No exercise in sensuality, Amis's concordance of kisses adds little to our knowledge of kissing. What it does do is reinforce the stereotype of the sexually precocious manipulative Jewish bitch.

The unrepressed sexuality of the vamp and the vampire make them potent symbols in a culture like ours which has a love–hate relationship with sex. Perversely, however, the best-known kiss in Western culture is not a kiss of sexual love or sexual transgression. It is the one that Judas is said to have bestowed on Jesus. The kiss of Judas and the uses to which it has been put reveal more about humanity than perhaps we would like to know.

The Devil's Advocate

Judas has been damned by history for carrying out what the Bible and hundreds of years of theology tell us was the will of God. 'In the case of Judas,' writes Augustine, 'what great good did he!' God punished him anyway, making the word Judas synonymous with betrayal, but, said Augustine, the faithful should not worry their heads about such contradictions, 'For the mysteries which lie hidden in Scripture, no one who is content with the simplicity of faith would curiously sift them . . . heretics cavil.'

Let's cavil.

It is hard to find anything good to say about Judas, but it is salutary to remember that there are three betrayals in the story: that of Jesus, that of Judas, and that of the very idea of the kiss which is perverted into its opposite. Let us begin at the beginning, with cannibalism and its codification into sacrifice.

A taste for the taste of human flesh, revenge, and the only viable alternative to starvation are documented motives for human cannibalism. There is also the magical belief that in eating the body the diner ingests the victim's courage and strength. Survival and magic were key factors in the sacrifice of Jesus. Christianity would live and humanity would acquire his virtues and be redeemed. Although no one literally ate Jesus's flesh, symbolic cannibalism is central to Christian ritual and myth.

The idea of sacrifice, so fundamental to the doctrines of Hinduism, Islam, Judaism and Christianity, may have arisen from the sharing of meat in prehistoric times. Hunters shared the day's catch with each other. Later, when they had flocks of sheep, the meat and the blood were shared with the gods. Great heroes have always proclaimed their achievements with feasts in which the assembled celebrants partook of a human's or beast's body and blood.

At a fraternity party I once attended in California, a pit was dug into the earth, lined with stones, and a pig was roasted. When the pig was cooked, it was torn to pieces and eaten lustily, with the juices running from our mouths. Ours was a rather nonsensical slaughter, a sacrament of youth; but ritual slaughter has a codified sacramental function in many religions.

Stories such as Jesus's are common in mythology – in the mystery cults of Osiris, Attis and Adonis – a close bond often existing between the sacrificial victim and the slayer. Week-long celebrations of Attis took place every year at about the time now celebrated as Easter. A triumphal procession with a man enthroned, representing Attis, culminated in his death, the death of the god. After Jesus's death, through the influence of Paul, he was transformed from an itinerant Jewish preacher into a mystery-god.

Paul, whose authenticated Epistles are the earliest writings in the New Testament, does not seem to know of Judas's treachery. The betrayal by Judas was added to the story later, his kiss becoming the first morsel in the cannibalism of Jesus.

Like a cook pressing his lips to the spoon, tasting the simmering dish he is roasting, Judas symbolically tastes the flesh of Jesus. Kissing, remember, is mock-eating – it shows trust because one allows the other to come close enough to eat one's flesh, but taboos against cannibalism (and hurting friends) prevent it. Kissing is eating without devouring.

It is no accident, either, I believe, that chewing was banned in the taking of the body in the Eucharist. And yet the wafer is consumed. Indeed, the crime is felt to be so great that in the Mass one must re-enact and again and again be rendered guiltless of the murder of Christ.

Just occasionally, religious fanatics misunderstand, and kill to drink the blood of the lamb. John Haigh, who murdered nine people and drank their blood, was sentenced to death in Lewes, England, in 1949. Haigh, who had won a divinity prize at the age of seventeen, was tormented by the idea of Jesus's long suffering on the cross. He made sure his nine victims died quickly and with no foreknowledge, shooting or clubbing them from behind.

Deeply impressed by the idea of salvation through drinking the blood of the lamb, he had recurring dreams about drinking blood, and when he had a car accident in which he was hurt and his own blood dripped into his mouth, he decided it was 'divine guidance'. After each murder, Haigh slashed the victim's neck with a penknife to open the jugular vein and draw a glassful of blood which he drank down.

At the Last Supper, Jesus made the symbolic offering of his body and his blood; but to live, Christianity required the more dramatic sacrifice of the real thing. Unless Jesus died, there would be no salvation. His death, therefore, was desired by those hungry for redemption. Giving in to blood lust, for whatever reason, occasioned great guilt, as it would among any normal group of people. So, someone other than the beneficiaries had to be blamed. In the Epistles written by

Paul himself, the blame is not fixed. Later, as the story was retold in the Gospels, a scapegoat appeared: Judas, whose betrayal was added to the story in these later versions. He carries the guilt for Christendom.

The four Gospels, written long after the death of Jesus, contradict each other on some points, but tell much the same tale. At the Last Supper Jesus predicted his betrayal, and after the Last Supper he and the twelve apostles made their way to the Garden of Gethsemane. Jesus thought the betrayal necessary, and made sure no one impeded it. Judas Iscariot, one of his disciples, who had put himself at the service of the enemies of Jesus as an informer, arrived with a band of men who intended to arrest Jesus as soon as they knew which one he was. The signal was to be a kiss of greeting. On arriving Judas said, 'Master, master,' and kissed him.

Like all kisses, this was a kiss that identified the special one; but this kiss, cynically, inverted the very point of kissing. Not only was Judas Iscariot's kiss a betrayal of Christ, it was a betrayal of the meanings signified by the gesture itself, a prostitution of a gesture we hold to be friendly or loving. 'Faithful are the wounds of a friend,' says the Old Testament, 'but the kisses of an enemy are deceitful' (Proverbs 27:6).

Judas's kiss is not the only kiss of death in the scriptures. In the Old Testament, in the midst of a kiss of salutation, a greeting such as the one Judas was supposed to be giving Jesus, General Joab kills his rival Amasa with his sword:

And Joab said to Amasa, Art thou in health, my brother? And Joab took Amasa by the beard with the right hand to kiss him.

But Amasa took no heed to the sword that was in Joab's hand: so he smote him therewith in the fifth rib, and shed out his bowels to the ground, and struck him not again; and he died. (II Samuel 20: 9–10)

Nor is Judas's the only kiss of betrayal. By masquerading as his brother, Jacob steals Esau's inheritance with a kiss:

And his father Isaac said unto him, Come near now, and kiss me, my son. And he came near, and kissed him: and he smelled the smell of his raiment, and blessed him. (Genesis 27: 26–7)

As in the case of Joab, the kiss of Judas leads to murder; as in the case of Jacob, it uses guile.

The first account of the story of Judas and Jesus, although not the first in the Bible, was written in about AD 70 by Mark. Mark's Gospel suggests that Jesus knew that the betrayal would happen, but took no steps to elude it. In the midst of the Last Supper, 'as they sat and did eat, Jesus said, Verily I say unto you, One of you which eateth with me shall betray me' (Mark 14: 18).

It has been argued that Jesus and Judas were co-operating in the betrayal. It has even been suggested that Jesus *ordered* Judas to betray him so that Christianity might live. In John's version, when Jesus announces that 'one of you shall betray me', he is asked which one, and replies, the one to whom I give a piece of bread I have dipped in wine: 'And when he had dipped the sop, he gave it to Judas Iscariot, the son of Simon. And after the sop Satan entered into him. Then Jesus said unto him, That thou doest, do quickly' (John 13: 26–7).

In the Garden of Gethsemane, Jesus wakes the sleeping disciples so that he can keep his rendezvous with fate: 'Rise up, let us go; lo, he that betrayeth me is at hand' (Mark 14: 42). Finally, the moment of betrayal arrives. Judas steps forward from the multitude who are carrying swords and staves: 'And he that betrayed him had given them a token, saying, Whomsoever I shall kiss, that same is he; take him, and lead him away safely. And as soon as he was come, he goeth straightway to him, and saith, Master, master; and kissed him. And they laid their hands on him, and took him' (Mark 14: 43–6).

When one of Jesus's men attempts to resist, slicing off the ear of an attacker, Jesus makes the famous he who lives by the sword dies by the sword pronouncement and explains that the arrest is in fact his own choice: 'Thinkest thou that I cannot now pray to my Father, and he shall presently give me more than twelve legions of angels? But how then shall the scriptures be fulfilled?' (Matthew 26: 53–4). In John's Gospel, too, he dramatically halts all resistance, and opts to face his destiny: 'Put up thy sword into the sheath: the cup which my Father hath given me, shall I not drink it?' (John 18: 11).

Some scholars have wondered why Jesus needed identifying. He had been preaching openly in Jerusalem, and he was well enough known to warrant action being taken against him. This issue once so worried Christians that in his twelfth-century blockbuster, *The Golden Legend*, Jacopus de Voragine makes the case that Judas's kiss was necessary to distinguish him from James, the Lord's brother, who looked very like him. Others have said that the soldiers in question were newly arrived from Rome. In which case, wouldn't it have been easier and potentially less dangerous for Judas to have given the soldiers directions, or guided them to the entrance of the garden, or, if he had to get close, simply to have pointed at Jesus?

But a Judas who pointed a distant finger would not be so dramatic a scapegoat as one who betrayed with a kiss. The kiss does wonders for the story. It shows an intimacy between the good man and the incarnation of evil, between the one who is to be sacrificed and the one who leads the lamb to the slaughter. In Luke's Gospel as Judas draws near, Jesus says: 'Judas, betrayest thou the Son of man with a kiss?' Like a black mass, the kiss betrays because it is an inversion of good. If Judas had betrayed Jesus with a handshake, we would not have such a powerful symbol.

There is some question as to the nature of the kiss between Judas and Jesus. This kiss, which may never actually have happened, has been the subject of much dispute. Although *The Golden Legend*'s medieval author seems convinced that Jesus was kissed on the face, to show reverence or respect, Judas might have kissed Jesus on the foot, on the hand, or on the hem of his robe. Or, as in the kiss between Joab and Amasa – which may have given Mark the idea of adding a kiss to the story of Jesus – Judas might have kissed his face with a hand under the beard. An analysis of the Greek of the Bible by Kirk Hughes suggests that the kiss may well have been on the face, even on the lips, as it was one of intensity rather than mere reverence (or simulated reverence): 'At the moment, Judas "kissed" him (kataphileō; Matt 26: 49; Mark 14: 45). His kissing (phileō) intensifies (kataphileō; Luke 7: 38, 45, 15: 20; Acts 20: 37). This is all the Gospels say. Two lips at least, but maybe four. Judas could have kissed his mouth.' The one who felt the intensity, however, might have been the author of the Gospel rather than the authors of the kiss.

Was Judas a secret agent? A kind of Scarlet Pimpernel? The twentieth century's most scholarly great writer, Jorge Luis Borges, once said of Judas – the agent of redemption – 'A man whom the Redeemer has thus distinguished deserves from us the best interpretations of his deeds'. He has not received it. To call someone 'a Judas' today is to call him a traitor. The sheep or cow that leads the others to the slaughter is called the Judas; so is any animal used to trap others of its species. The method of turning quail into Judases turns the stomach. A quail is captured, then blinded and put in a cage. It whimpers in pain, and these distress calls soon bring the other quail, who are killed. A Judas hole is the name prisoners have given to the peephole in a prison door through which the guard looks to spy on them.

'We would not name a child or even a dog Judas,' muses the scholar George Buttrick. 'Yet it is a good name. It comes from Judah, it means worthy-to-be-praised.' No longer.

To bestow the kiss of death also has a metaphorical meaning: that of voicing approval which guarantees failure.

The betrayal by Judas continues to be regarded as one of the most dastardly crimes on record; but, if one reads carefully, the culprit seems to be Jesus. He sets Judas up to do it, and wants it done, so that the scriptures might be fulfilled. Jesus knew that whoever was God's instrument in effecting the 'betrayal' would become a scapegoat. Thus, *he* betrayed *Judas*.

The fate of Judas varies from gospel to gospel. Most commentators believe that he did it for the money, with which, we read in Luke's sequel Acts, he bought a field. But there was to be no peaceful agricultural life for Judas: his wickedness engorges his body till it spurts open and his innards gush out. *The Golden Legend* embroidered the blood and guts of Acts but, with a marvellous nicety of feeling, refused to let anything hideous happen to the mouth which had kissed Jesus. Judas 'burst asunder in the midst, and all his bowels gushed out'. But 'he did not vomit them from the mouth, because his mouth could not be defiled, having touched the glorious face of Christ.'

Satan enters the plot for the first time in the two later gospels, those of Luke and John. Now it is Satan, not God the Father, who ordains Jesus's death; Judas has become the agent of Satan. 'Then entered Satan into Judas surnamed Iscariot, being of the number of twelve,' writes Luke. 'And he went his way, and communed with the chief priests and captains, how he might betray him unto them' (Luke 22: 3–4).

Satan may well have been added to the plot because it was noticed that to blame Judas for what God ordained was both unfair and irrational. The last Gospel, that of John, makes many errors or changes thought to be useful. In John, it is not Judas alone who is guilty but 'the Jews'. In self-defence, in about AD 250, the Talmud offered a reinterpretation of the story. The plot remains essentially that of Mark and Matthew, including the kiss, but here Jesus is a sorcerer, seducing the credulous to idolatry, and Judas a brave undercover agent. In the finale, Judas foils attempts to foster a belief in the resurrection by producing the body of Jesus, which hangs on a cabbage-stalk in Judas's garden. This version never caught on. Even among practising Jews it is not well known. And over the centuries, Judas and his namesakes the Jews (defined as Judas's, not Jesus's, people) became *personae non gratae* in Christendom.

Christians, whose God was supposed to be the God of love, found it hard to live with their guilt at the human sacrifice, the murder, that had made their religion live. So great was their guilt that the instrument of Jesus's death was demonized, and the kiss of Judas became a reason to oppress the Jews. The scholar Hyam Maccoby, analyses this development in his book *Judas Iscariot and the Myth of Jewish Evil*. 'The people who most ardently desire the death, because they believe with perfect faith that it brings them salvation, are stricken by grief and horror when it occurs ... The deeper the grief, the more the community of Christians disassociate themselves from the death which they desired, the more Judas, the scapegoat, is blamed.' Judas, Maccoby says, was 'delegated' to murder Jesus on their behalf. 'By washing their hands like Pilate, and mourning and bewailing the death of Jesus every Easter, they hope to avoid complicity in his death. The more they cover Judas and the Jews with obloquy and hatred, the more they can distance themselves from responsibility.'

So, decent people could behave indecently to no longer quite human Jews with impunity. Anthropologists have a concept useful here, which they call pseudospeciation. 'Pseudo' means false; 'speciation' means the making of a new species, unique genetically, which happens by evolution over time. In pseudospeciation, the changes are not genetic. Distinct customs and ideas within a group, handed down from each generation to the next, give a group the false notion that they are virtually a separate species. Pseudospeciation in humans means that the group not only regards itself as very different from another group, but applies different standards of behaviour in its dealings with that other group. Members of the in-group are provided with food and shelter, for example, whereas members of the out-group are robbed. In its extreme form, pseudospeciation leads to the dehumanizing of other groups. Not only are the out-group regarded as non-human, they may even be hurt or killed without inhibition. Chimpanzees do it too: most babies are protected by adults, but a baby that comes from another troop is 'dechimpized' – and murdered in the same manner as a prey animal.

In humans, this happens for brief periods when there is warfare, and for longer periods when there is prejudice. All of us are less inhibited when it comes to showing anger to strangers, and to some extent, even the most tolerant and best-mannered humans dehumanize other drivers on the road. In London, not long ago, a friend in whose car I was riding began to curse an aggressive motorist who was trying to cut in, only to realize it was someone she knew.

Immediately, her anger vanished, and my friend smiled and blew a kiss to the other driver.

As time went on, the story of the capture of Jesus was refashioned so that the Jews might be demonized, dehumanized, pseudospeciated. This was safer than attacking the powerful Romans.

The fresco by Giotto (1276–1377) of *The Kiss of Judas* shows the two men face to face, with Judas's arms around the shoulders of Jesus who is entirely enveloped by Judas's long cloak. A thick-featured Judas – Neanderthal? leprous? – leans forward to bestow the kiss, whereas Jesus remains upright. Or perhaps Giotto has depicted the moment just after the kiss, when his stern-eyed Jesus who is looking Judas in the eye realizes that both their fates are sealed.

The Taking of Christ by Caravaggio, painted 300 years later, gives a similar impression. Judas is grasping Jesus's upper arm firmly as if they are about to embrace or have just released one another from the embrace. Judas's face is dark, his features crude. Jesus and Judas are looking at one another intently. The lips of both are pursed. One is very aware of the mouths. The kiss of betrayal hangs in the air.

In the passion plays, Judas had red hair, the same colour as the devil, and wore a yellow robe, which in medieval symbolism stood for treachery. It was perhaps no accident that the Nazis chose a yellow badge for the Jews.

The novel *The Statement* by Brian Moore, published in 1995, is set in contemporary France, where a septuagenarian French Nazi war criminal suddenly suspects that the abbeys and monasteries which have protected him for half a century have joined forces with his enemies: 'And then the Abbot said, "Pierre, I feel badly about this, but . . . I don't feel I can offer you a bed, not even for tonight. However, I'll be happy to help you financially."'

The war criminal refuses the money. 'Pray for me,' he says.

The Abbot opened the heavy front door and, as so often in the past, clasped him briefly in a farewell embrace. 'Safe journey, Pierre.'

'The Judas kiss . . .'

As I walk away now, I know he's watching, waiting to see how I take his betrayal. Step out like a soldier. Left, Right, Left, Right.

Like the traitorous abbot, Mafia bosses are said to perpetuate the kiss of death; in *Godfather II*, Michael Corleone kisses Fredo on the lips, soon sending him to his death. If it is true that Mafia bosses have been told to stop kissing in public because it gives their identity away, this movie genre will need not only to invent a new symbol of brotherhood but to find one that will horrify us equally. A handshake of betrayal lacks impact. And it is hard to imagine any symbol other than the kiss which, if used as an instrument of betrayal, would so appal us.

The kiss of Judas leaves a bitter taste in the mouth. Apparently innocent social kisses can be just as wily. Our chimpanzee cousins probably engage in them instinctively. So, as I one day found out, do humans.

RITES BESEECHING PASSAGE

Norman Mailer kissed me when I arrived to interview him.
'I remember you,' the aged silver-back gorilla of American
letters said when he saw me at the door of his hotel suite,
and pecked me on the cheek. I was under no illusions. The
kiss was to encourage me to be gentle with him in *The Times*.
A year or so before, I had interviewed him for a magazine,
and my piece had been hostile. This time he wanted to
disarm me. Placating with kisses, as many species know,
reduces tension, keeps the stronger sweet, appeases for the
moment and acknowledges the status quo.

Apes do it, fish do it, even Churchmen do it, and of course
the French do it. Parisians greet each other with a kiss on
both cheeks, but in warmer Provence it is a minimum of
three. East European leaders (if on speaking terms) press their
fleshy cheeks. The Soviet president Brezhnev famously kissed
the East German president Honecker on the lips, officially
designating him an equal; which of course he was not. The
kiss established temporary ritual equality.

Proclaiming ritual *in*equality with a kiss can be just as

reassuring, because it announces mutual acceptance of the status quo. The ostensible purpose of kissing the Pope's ring, for example, may be to show reverence for him as a representative of God, but it is also a show of willing submission to his temporal authority. Once acknowledged, power need not be acted out. When a powerful, sharp-toothed male chimpanzee shows his imminent displeasure, a nearby female, being smaller, sidles up and plants a kiss. Weaker males do it too. Dominant females receive the same treatment. Kissing is a standard 'pattern of submission' among our closest relatives. A kiss of appeasement is, like a kiss of greeting, good preventative medicine.

Primates seem to understand this instinctively, as a young gorilla called Julia once demonstrated to me in the Abuko nature reserve in the Gambia. Julia was being rehabilitated to return to the wild. She was just old enough to begin to be dangerous. Her trainer always carried a sharp machete just in case. While high in the trees, the red colobus monkeys were grooming their infants by licking and kissing away the twigs in their fur, I played in a dirt clearing with the orphan gorilla.

It was very like playing with a two-year-old human. Julia would run at me, trusting that I wanted her whether my arms were open or not, but she was so strong that when we collided she could knock me down. Once she grasped my hand and we ran together; she was too fast and I fell, but she kept running and was so strong I could not disentangle my fingers. She dragged me a short way. If she had wanted to, the gorilla could have hurt me seriously. Instead, as I lay on the ground, Julia kissed me, brushing her open lips against my cheek, somewhat like a dog licking her owner's face. At the time, I thought Julia's kiss was high spirits or affection. I was taller than Julia, but lighter, and she was unquestionably the stronger. Perhaps, though, she understood more about the machete than I realized. Or maybe she was placating me because she wanted the game to go on.

The psychiatrist D. W. Winnicott described an incident of seemingly instinctive human appeasement behaviour. His four-year-old patient Gabrielle, less outgoing than her younger sister, was less successful socially: 'Strangers take more readily to her sister Susan, who is curly-haired, extroverted and cheeky, than to the long inquiring looks of Gabrielle,' her parents wrote to the psychiatrist. 'Gabrielle is very close to Susan, handles her with great circumspection. We are struck by how often she will try and get her way by deflecting Susan's attention or by some inventiveness, rather than by direct attack. The other day, in the middle of a fierce fight, she suddenly kissed Susan and said: "But I like you."'

This is appeasement; unsubtle, too. It is designed, like all appeasement behaviour, not only to soothe the stronger enemy and dissuade her from invading geographical or emotional territory, but also to put the appeaser at ease. 'Let's kiss and make up,' Gabrielle was saying non-verbally.

Perhaps Norman Mailer kissed me by instinct rather than intent. Or perhaps it originated as instinct and after he had done it to a few journalists it became a useful tool. It seems possible that as a category the kiss of greeting originated in much this way: individual desire to keep things amiable was codified into social ritual. Both the cultivated gorilla and the wild one pecked me on the cheek. If we were French it would have been both cheeks. Had it been centuries ago and I that distinguished primate the Emperor of all Rome would they instead have kissed my hand?

Where you plant the kiss has long depended on your social position relative to the person you are greeting. But whether it signals equality or unequal social rank, a kiss of greeting signifies acquiescence in the status quo, and therefore is a ritual of reassurance. Difficulties can occur, though, if one misreads the cultural code, or uses the code of one culture or sub-culture to communicate with another. When Queen Elizabeth arrived, a slum dweller in Washington DC exuberantly hugged and kissed her hello – friendliness in the Washingtonian's world; a breach of protocol in the queen's. One doesn't kiss the queen at all. One bows or curtseys, symbolically (and actually) enacting the inferiority of social position, lowering oneself. Few other persons' persons remain so sacred.

Historically, the lower your status the more distant from the face your kiss has tended to be. Equals might kiss each other on the mouth or cheek, but you kissed those above you on the hand, those more powerful still on the knee, and the highest of all on the foot. One abases oneself by bending so low. Like kissing someone's foot, kissing the ground bares your back. It is a symbolic enactment of your inferior position and a restatement of your vulnerability to the more powerful one. The Pope's many encounters with the ground can be understood in this light. When the Pope kisses the earth on landing from his plane, he is baring his back to God and showing reverence for his creation. He may also just be pleased to be back on terra firma.

Kisses of greeting are in a sense rites beseeching passage, and they signify that the two greeters are on amicable terms and occupy a safe space. Proximity makes one physically vulnerable; acceding to it signals trust. The chimpanzee trusts that despite putting herself in the power of another, she will not be bitten. The human trusts that unlike the biblical King David's general Amasa, he will not be stabbed in the belly in mid-kiss, nor in the back. This implicit trust is one reason why kisses of betrayal so electrify our imagination.

Herodotus (c.484–425 BC) mentions that the Persians greeted each other with a kiss. Equals kissed on the mouth, others on the cheek. The Bible tends to be less specific as to the exact nature of the kiss of greeting: 'And the Lord said to Aaron, Go into the wilderness to meet Moses. And he went, and met him in the mount of God, and kissed him.' The Bible speaks of Jewish equals kissing in greeting after first each placing a hand underneath the other's beard: 'And Joab took Amasa by the beard with the right hand to kiss him.' The beard itself might be kissed. Other signs of reverence were kissing the hem of the revered one's garment or kissing his feet, as Mary Magdalen did Christ's.

In classical Greece one kissed the hand, the knee, the breast of a social superior. Vase paintings suggest that Greeks also on occasion touched their fingers to their own lips. To show admiration, present-day Spaniards, Italians and Greeks kiss their fingertips. Historians of gesture speculate that this fingertip kiss may have originated in ancient Greece.

In ancient Rome, there were three major categories of kisses. *Osculum* was the kiss of friendship on the face or cheek, *basium* the kiss of affection on the lips, and *suavium* the lovers' kiss. One greeted images of the gods by kissing your own hand and blowing a kiss towards the icon. Is there something innate in this kiss of reverence, or is it just coincidence that the Aztecs had a similar ritual kiss? Mexico had not been exposed to the culture of Rome, but when the explorer Cortez, whom the Aztecs regarded as a god, arrived and bowed to Montezuma, he replied by dropping his hand to the ground and then bringing it up to his lips. The Aztec ruler was symbolically kissing the ground.

A Roman emperor, however, daintily held out his hand to be kissed. Caligula, the insane, used to cause deliberate insult by extending just his middle finger to be kissed. Then as now it was a rude gesture. A dominant chimpanzee also offers his hand to a lower-ranking one who touches it with his mouth.

Chimpanzees also kiss when they have made a kill. What looks to us like murderous pleasure is probably just a way of reassuring one another after the violence, a way of rebonding. He's dead, it says, but you're all right, Jack. You're one of us. Eat up.

One motto of the early Christians was, 'Greet all the brethren with a holy kiss.' When the Crusaders kissed the cross before battle it was not a salutation, but a ritual of reassurance.

That other preoccupation of medieval knights, kissing dragons, is not quite the rage it used to be. The idea that a kiss could deliver someone from monstrousness enthralled medieval audiences. It works for us too. Transforming monsters – or at any rate dangerous acquaintances – into more malleable friends is one of the hidden agendas in ordinary everyday kisses of greeting. Each time we kiss a friend or a business acquaintance hello, we kiss and tame the foul and fiery mouth of the dragon.

The successful export of the social, cheek-to-cheek kiss from France to the rest of Europe in recent years is one of the few uncontested successes of the European Community. What some historians say originated as a rural French habit was transported to urban France and then to the rest of Europe. Originally, French peasants took hold of each other's shoulders and kissed cheeks noisily, heartily – the affection could be measured by the decibel level. In urban culture, though, just as a neighbour's stereo is more acceptable if muted, so are the sounds of the body. The social kiss is quiet now.

It is also much less physical. This would appear to be an instance of gestural gentrification. In many gestures, less movement has long been thought more elegant. In France, as elsewhere, in kisses of greeting the lips never quite touch the cheek. Nor, usually, do the cheeks quite touch. To touch cheeks with someone one hardly knows during a kiss is one way of flirting.

In southern Europe, men and women often greet each other with the cheek kiss whether they are close friends or not. In the north, the gesture is usually limited to people who know each other fairly well, although kissing is definitely on the increase. The Dutch still have misunderstandings about the number of cheeks to kiss in the greeting ritual, but the British, other northern Europeans and Americans seem quite clear about it, limiting the number of cheeks to one. Women kiss the air in the vicinity of the cheek of everyone; men only kiss friends or colleagues of the other sex. But seeing an American, a European or a Yanomami father playfully air-kissing his child of either sex is quite an ordinary sight. These exuberant kisses in the air, not quite touching the face, welcoming the baby to emotional intimacy, are further evidence of the kiss continuum.

The French were not always at the top of the kissing hierarchy. In fact, at one time the English may have dominated the scene. In 1466 a visiting Bohemian nobleman called Leo von Rozmital claimed that guests arriving at an English inn would be met by their hostess and her family who would 'go out to meet and receive them; and the guests are required to kiss them all. This among the English,' he said, is 'the same as shaking hands among the other nations.' Thirty years later, the learned and much respected scholar Erasmus wrote a letter to his friend Fausto Andrelini urging him to come to England because the women were pretty and very kissable. 'There is a custom here never to be sufficiently commended. When ever you come you are received with a kiss by all; when you take your leave, you are dismissed with kisses again; they leave you, you kiss them all around. Should you meet anywhere, kisses in abundance; in fine, wherever you move, there is nothing but kisses.' Half a century later, the kissing hadn't stopped. The Greek traveller Nicander Nucius, who visited England in 1545, noticed that even men and women who were virtual strangers greeted each other with kisses on the lips. 'They display great simplicity and absence of jealousy in their usages towards females. For not only do those who are of the same family and household kiss them on the mouth with salutations and embraces, but even those too who have never seen them.' During this period dresses were extremely low-cut, and a man might show even greater cordiality to his 'kissing kin' by putting his hand casually on her breast. As the century waned, so did kissing.

Is it possible that Erasmus and the Czech nobleman were confusing the *demi-monde* with polite society? In any event, a century later things had certainly changed. Thomas Coryate, an English visitor to Italy, noticed 'an extraordinary custom', 'that when two acquaintances meet 'they give a mutual kiss' which they repeat when they depart from each other.' His book *Crudities*, published in 1611, is scathing about the gesticulating Italians.

In England, by the end of the seventeenth century, the kiss of greeting was for the most part restricted to lovers, and to parents and their children. The Restoration had introduced the English court to 'fine reserved airs' of the French, who preferred bowing to kissing. 'You think you're in the country where great lubberly brothers slabber and kiss one another when they meet, like a call of Sergeants,' says a character in Congreve's *The Way of the World* (1700). ''Tis not the fashion here.' Another of Congreve's plays, *Love For Love*, contains the famous phrase 'kiss and tell': 'Oh, fie, Miss, you must not kiss and tell.'

Every nationality seems to think the grass is more lubricious on the other side of the frontier. In many Polish manors of the sixteenth century a servant would be posted in a treetop to watch the road so that he could announce the approach of visitors and the family could assemble to greet them at the door. This welcoming ritual began with bowing and embracing in front of the doors. The visitor would hand over his sword to be placed in a corner, and a servant would arrive with bottles and a glass on a tray; the glass was emptied amid much hugging and kissing.

In the seventeenth century, though, Poles seemed to be looking backward. 'Two people of the same social standing would embrace and kiss each other on the shoulders; subordinates are expected to kiss the knees, calves or feet of their superiors,' wrote a Frenchman visiting Poland in the second half of the century. The chest and stomach of a powerful patron might also be kissed; also his hand.

Like waltzing, hand-kissing has become in the last few centuries a highly stylized, formal, male–female interaction which hints at a sexual connotation, one more obvious than in most other kisses of greeting, even though they are to the face.

This cross-over is very evident in the film of Edith Wharton's *The Age of Innocence*, which is set in over-starched, 1870s New York. Constrained by convention from going further, the hero, played by Daniel Day Lewis, lingeringly presses his lips against the back of Michelle Pfeiffer's gloved hand, imbuing the kiss with intense desire.

'First time he kiss'd me,' recalls the nineteenth-century English poet Elizabeth Barrett Browning in *Sonnets from the Portuguese*,

> he but only kiss'd
> The fingers of this hand wherewith I write;
> And ever since it grew more clean and white.

In Eastern Europe hand-kissing is still practised, although sometimes with a certain sense of irony; and in Austria one still sometimes hears the salutation, 'I kiss your hand, gracious lady.'

The hand is correctly kissed on slightly bended knee, the man bending forward to reach the extended hand. The French statesman Giscard d'Estaing was expert. Photographs of him kissing the hand of Queen Farah of Iran, quite some years ago now, show duly bent head. But, at a formal reception in Bucharest, the American actress and ambassador Shirley Temple Black was bemused when a Romanian diplomat snared his red beard in her ring.

A decade ago the *Wall Street Journal*, discovering a new corporate trend, devoted 46 column inches to the subject of the business kiss. On Madison Avenue in 1988, to kiss or not to kiss was a vexing question. Was it condescendingly sexist, executives wondered, or presumptuously intrusive, or merely warmly and sophisticatedly European? In London, *The Times*, although purportedly amused at the Americans, responded with 20 column inches. 'Nothing illustrates more the insincerity of mixing business and personal relationships than the hypocritical kiss,' Peter Gorb of the London Business School said emphatically. 'I don't like the assumption of personal intimacy.'

Although air-kissing is now acceptable, indeed mandatory, in many corporate spheres, kissing is still sometimes a vexing question. In London, recently, I dined with an urbane American whose business dealings often took him to Europe. It was a pleasant evening, at the end of which, as the taxi pulled up to take me away, I stood on tiptoe to peck him in the air in the vicinity of the cheek at the very moment that he took my hand into his to shake. This dissonance in our sense of social ritual left us both embarrassed, me feeling like one of those bad foreign women in a Henry James novel, enticing the innocent American.

On both sides of the Atlantic, it is still social convention that when you come upon two people kissing you look away. Except at the movies. The movies teach us how to kiss, give us a model of desire and romance, and allow what anywhere else would be the most shameful voyeurism.

PHALLIC THROATS AND THRUSTING ARMS

It was instinct or cynicism, not a conscious aesthetic, which led early movie-makers to exploit the possibilities of kissing. The clinch scene very soon became obligatory. As the song says:

> The movies, the movies, that fabulous blend
> Of laughter, adventure, the kiss at the end . . .

The movies had practically begun with a kiss – *The Kiss*. Thirty seconds long, the film with the first screen kiss consisted entirely of a man and a woman kissing in close-up. It was shot in the springtime of 1896 by the Edison Company and went on immediate release. Its full title was *The May Irwin–John C. Rice Kiss*. The principals, professional stage actors, originally performed it on Broadway as a brief scene in the hit comedy, *The Widow Jones*. Rice, who had a Daliesque waxed handlebar mustache, took Irwin's nondescript face in his hands, pressed his unparted lips against hers, and produced a stream of baby kisses. Irwin did little but seem to like it. Audiences loved it. As the film toured America, reviews were good and receipts were sizeable.

The first trouble came in June when it opened in Chicago. There it vastly offended the critic Herbert S. Stone: 'Neither participant is physically attractive, and the spectacle of their prolonged pasturing on each other's lips was hard to bear when only life size. Magnified to Gargantuan proportions and repeated three times over it is absolutely disgusting,' he fulminated. 'While we tolerate such things, what avails all the talk of American Puritanism and of the filthiness of imported English and French stage shows?' This, the first of what would be many calls for movie censorship, went unheeded. *The Kiss* continued to play until the celluloid reels fell apart.

In London's Leicester Square that same year, on the roof of the Alhambra Theatre, two actors were filmed kissing in *The Soldier's Courtship*, another adaptation of a stage comedy. The stars were Fred Storey and Julie Seale. More sex on screen in which the kiss figured prominently followed very rapidly. In Paris that November, Eugène Pirou, the pioneering producer of sex exploitation films, screened *The Bride Goes to Bed/Le Coucher de la mariée* in the basement of the Café de Paris. The story of how very carefully newly-weds undress for bed, the three-minute movie has a Cinderella moment in which the husband removes his bride's satin slipper and presses it to his lips.

Like most successful artists and all able businessmen, the earliest movie moguls realized quickly that sex sells. In *The Story the Biograph Told* (1903) an office boy photographs a husband kissing his secretary; the wife, seeing the evidence, ends the infidelity, morality – or rather, convention – triumphing only after we have had our thrill.

There was plenty of mush too – a preponderance of sweetness and artificially constructed moral light – as in *Young Romance* (1915), in which two department store clerks who have never met (he is in hardware, she in notions) hoping to find love on a higher social scale pose as wealthy socialites at a summer resort. Instead they fall in love with each other and the movie becomes, as so many others were to do, a paean to ordinary life. Adapted from a story by the period's foremost sentimentalist O. Henry, it ends with a kiss. This plot – boy discovers girl next door and they live happily and self-satisfiedly ever after – would be one of the movies' main story-lines for the next three-quarters of a century.

But there was no censorship, and in the silents often anything went. In the forty years of movie-making that preceded the inception of strict official censorship there were some remarkably frank movies touching on the issues of abortion, prostitution and adultery, subjects which would later be curtailed or banned. A 1912 film showed the first frontal male nude scene, and early pornographic films included masturbation, anal sex and fellatio. Rudolph Valentino, the Sheik, ravaged maidens; Theda Bara's and Garbo's vamps delivered transgressive kisses of moral death. In 1922, in an orgy scene in Cecil B. DeMille's *Manslaughter*, came the first lascivious kiss between two members of the same sex. In 1930, in *Morocco,* Marlene Dietrich became the first leading lady to kiss another woman. Playing a nightclub singer so earnestly in love with Foreign Legionnaire Gary Cooper that she follows him into the desert on foot in high heels, Dietrich paused in mid-plot to don top hat and tails and provocatively kiss the lips of an attractive woman. The famous German film *Mädchen in Uniform,* with its lesbian schoolgirls, was not released until a year later. In *Ecstasy* in 1933, Hedy Lamarr simulated an orgasm on the screen. The Czech film played even in Boston.

The following year the Hays Code intervened, banning

'excessive and lustful kissing, lustful embraces, suggestive postures and gestures', and a lot more besides. Hollywood, in much the same situation as today – with an outraged, conservative minority clamouring for a tightening of moral standards – instituted censorship voluntarily to forestall even stricter regulation. For nearly a dozen years, censorship had been a sham of Hays' 'Don'ts' and 'Be Carefuls'. Now it was very real. Under the Code, kisses in American films could no longer be horizontal: one had to be sitting or standing, not lying down; and in the movies, all married couples slept in twin beds. The 'treatment of bedrooms must be governed by good taste and delicacy', stated the Code. For at least a dozen years, kissing on a bed would be suspect. So were two people of opposite sexes on it. One of them had to have a foot on the floor.

The stars and the directors had not waited for an official code to develop a methodology of screen kissing. It was a craft, if not an art. Garbo had two kissing modes. In the first, her head thrown back in ecstasy, tilted at an angle of forty-five degrees to her body, she offers her face, offers her open lips; even this passivity had energy. In the second, she is the aggressor, her kisses devouring her leading man. She may be on top when she kisses, or else it is she who leans forward to initiate the kiss.

Often what is sexiest in the movies is the moment before the kiss, when the lips are hidden from the camera and we can imagine real kisses instead of the classically tight-lipped screen versions which outside of Hollywood were practised only by children. (Or so one hopes.) On screen, innocence was so sacred that many of the world's most kissable characters possessed it to a degree that veered into ineptitude: 'I love him,' Barbara Stanwyck says of Gary Cooper in *Ball of Fire*, 'because he doesn't know how to kiss – the jerk!'

The intensity of the kiss was communicated by stylized body language for which there is no official grammar. What I call the Phallic Throat was employed by leading ladies; the Thrusting Arm by leading men. Opposite Barrymore in *Grand Hotel*, Garbo's long, upturned neck, like Elizabeth Taylor's straining toward James Dean in *Giant*, became the visual phallic symbol. The Thrusting Arm was employed even by a clean-cut 'regular guy' like Jimmy Stewart. In *Ziegfeld Girl* (1941), when Stewart demands that Lana Turner leave her job as a showgirl because he is afraid he will lose her to a rich society playboy, she protests: 'I just gotta see it through.' Grasping his lapels, she looks up at him beseechingly. 'What'll I tell our grandkids if I don't?' Her body language is asking for a kiss. Instead, he turns his back on her and walks away, into the middle of the kiss scene, which, like the movie itself, had a beginning, a middle, and an end. After another exchange of B-movie quips, he turns to face her and the finale, in which he pulls her to him, making it clear that it is he who is doing the kissing, she the one kissed. Their lips are concealed by the back of Lana Turner's head. The emotion is conveyed by the forcefully Thrusting Arm.

The strong, long arm of the lawful husband, the would-be husband, or any of Hollywood's bad guys in the mood for love was the real action of many screen kisses, making the invisible kiss more exciting than those in which we saw pursed, childishly closed lips. So it was not the kiss that communicated passion; it was the armature of the kiss.

Gable was a master, crushing his leading lady to him so that her head or his obscured their lips, creating an illusion of passion without actually showing the kiss. The technique is very clear when he kisses his favourite leading lady Jean Harlow in *Hold Your Man* (1933). 'I think I'll give you a kiss,' he says, and does. In mid-kiss, he pulls her body into his, hard. One gets the sense of forceful joining from the violence of the arm, not the lips. He is the kisser, she the kissed.

When women are the kissers, men the kissees, one of two possibilities obtains. Either we are in the presence of depravity – the man is being vamped – or it is a moment of comedy. In *Ninotchka*, Garbo made kissing funny as well as sexy. She, a humourless, puritanical Russian commissar visiting Paris, and he (Melvyn Douglas), a middle-aged Count and playboy, are sitting on the floor of a hotel room, between two armchairs. 'But Ninotchka,' says Douglas, imploringly, 'Surely you feel some slight symptom of the divine passion, a burning of the lips that isn't thirst but something a thousand times more tantalizing more exalting than thirst?'

'You are very talkative,' Garbo replies.

He leans forward to kiss her, his head obscuring their lips. 'Was that talkative?' he asks.

'No, that was restful. Again.'

He complies. Then she pushes him forcefully against the armchair and kisses him rather more effectively. Throughout the scene, the kisses are obscured by the heads. The angle of her back, more pronounced than his was when he did the kissing, signals increasing tempestuousness. Her back functions exactly like the thrusting arm. Like the arm's, the back's incline is the angle of passion. We know her kiss is more effective, too, because Douglas, his lips parted expectantly, swooning, says, 'Again.' The audience is both titillated and, because of the role reversal, amused.

The Code imposed strict limitations on the duration of screen kisses, taxing the ingenuity even of master film-makers like Alfred Hitchcock. In his 1946 movie *Notorious,* coitus interruptus took on a new and subversive meaning. The kiss between Ingrid Bergman and Cary Grant, which begins on a balcony, is interrupted first when the telephone rings. There is intermittent nuzzling as they cross the room to answer the phone. The phone conversation is punctuated with a series of brief kisses which quickly build in intensity, though not in length, so that before long to the audience the telephone conversation becomes the punctuation of the kisses. It is at once funny and sexy. Hitchcock, determined to elude the censors, instructed the actors to 'Talk, kiss, talk, kiss.'

Bergman remembers, 'Hitchcock wanted to have a long kiss but that was forbidden; they stood over us with a watch and allowed us to kiss for a precise period – a very few seconds – before they told us to break it off.' With these interruptions, the kiss seems to go on and on but was never longer than a few seconds. The censor couldn't cut it. Hitchcock's aim, to elude the time limits of the Hays Code, worked, creating one of cinema's sexier kisses, among its funniest, and perhaps the most original, although *Don Juan*, in which John Barrymore and Mary Astor shared 127 kisses two decades earlier, still holds the record for the most in a single film.

No one is ever likely to break the all-time record for the longest kiss, held by Andy Warhol's art circuit movie *Kiss* (1963). The feature-length film consists entirely of Naomi Levine kissing Rufus Collins, Gerald Malanga and Ed Saunders. Its tediousness proves the maxim that more is less. Far more memorable is the 1988 film *Cinema Paradiso*'s final montage of clips which the local priest has demanded be censored. Here are some of the movies' greatest kiss scenes.

Not until the 1960s and the dawn of the age of the carnivore, however, would lips search, tongues stretch, or pairs of *orbicularis oris* muscles enter intense states of contraction. In Hollywood, lips would touch more in the manner of an iron on silk, tentatively, nervously, with anxiety lest one scorch the fabric.

The former American President Ronald Reagan, also a

former Hollywood leading man, has said that this non-kissing kissing was intentional: 'Actually the two people doing it were barely touching sometimes, in order to not push her face out of shape. You were doing it for the audience to see what in their minds they always think a kiss is.' 'Kissing . . . in the old days was very beautiful,' Reagan told NBC. 'Now you see a couple of people start chewing on each other.'

The battle for the reintroduction of nudity occupied the 1960s, and longer on-screen kisses came in this decade. In 1961, at the insistence of the censors, footage of Natalie Wood naked in *Splendor in the Grass* wound up on the cutting-room floor, but the movie made history for containing Hollywood's first French kiss. The man in question was a new generation's *homme fatal*, Warren Beatty. With the slackening of the Code, which was finally abolished in 1968, kisses became notably longer and their function changed. No longer did they have to stand in for orgasm. Faked orgasms were rife on the screen. Kisses now became kisses, and they could be voracious, tender, soppy or sweet. And once again they signify intimacy.

In *Pretty Woman* (1990), he is a millionaire businessman, she a streetwalker. A highly independent one. Instead of selling her body, she puts it under contract to him for six days and nights, first agreeing terms: 'I don't kiss on the mouth.'

'Neither do I,' he says.

Why not? Isn't it because we still believe that kisses unite souls? The kiss scene, when it happens, tells us it's love. It involves lots of little kisses, gentle, tender ones. Her friend, another prostitute, asks, Did you kiss? Even on the mouth? And when the answer is yes, she knows it's love.

Affairs to Remember

On the CBS-TV breakfast show the actor Kevin Kline described his movie *French Kiss* (1995) as 'an old-fashioned romantic comedy, boy meets girl, girl hates boy – then the opposites attract.' What really happens is that she changes her agenda for the future; he fulfils his. It all happens in the nicest possible way though. *French Kiss*, which really doesn't have any, is one of those schmaltzy movies you hate yourself for liking.

The kiss of recognition takes place when Meg Ryan, asleep and dreaming of kissing Charlie who has jilted her, just happens to kiss the French con-man Luc, played by Kline. Luc, wide awake, suddenly realizes he is in love with a squeaky clean American. She soon falls in love with Provence, where they decide to live happily ever after making wine and babies. The movie is about marriage, not sex, and is as squeaky clean as the heroine. For the sexiest kiss in the movies we must look elsewhere.

Gallup has already taken a poll. The sexiest kisses do not hail from the post-*Splendor in the Grass* age of the carnivore

169

but from the age of innocence when the Code had the studios in a moral armlock. According to the 1992 poll, the very sexiest kisses take place between Clark Gable and Vivien Leigh in *Gone With the Wind* (1939). Next come Burt Lancaster and Deborah Kerr in *From Here to Eternity* (1953), which gets my vote. Third are Bogart and Bergman in *Casablanca* (1942).

The most obvious explanation of the vote is that even though umpteen films showing more explicit kisses have been made in the last forty or fifty years, fewer people polled will have seen them. There are other reasons, too, why the big three have become kisses to remember.

In the film of *Gone With the Wind*, as he leaves for war, Rhett Butler tells Scarlett O'Hara: 'There's a soldier of the South who wants to love you, Scarlett, who wants to feel your arms around him, who wants to carry the memory of your kisses into battle with him. Never mind about loving me. Scarlett, kiss me, kiss me.'

They have just braved death in many terrifying guises – fire, explosion, men attempting to steal the horse and pull them from the carriage. They have even delivered the baby of the wife of the man Scarlett loves, a difficult delivery, of course – and now, suddenly, as the last semblance of law and order disappears with the retreating Confederate army, Rhett informs Scarlett that he is leaving to join the lost cause, leaving her amid the danger and the chaos with responsibility for the helpless mother and baby, and with God knows what other violent upheavals to expect. But Scarlett is supposed to respond to him.

Rhett pulls her down from the carriage – as the marauders so recently tried to – tells her he loves her, and then come those famous, purportedly romantic, lines. 'Scarlett, kiss me, kiss me.' When she doesn't, he forcibly kisses her. Afterwards, she upbraids him for not being a gentleman. In her failure to respond to him, we are supposed to see her lack of feeling for anyone but herself, her emotional shallowness. Why, I wonder, aren't we supposed to think just that of him? Not only has he been tremendously insensitive, his every statement to her is made in a supercilious, superior manner. That sixty years after it was filmed the movie is still so very popular can be attributed to those magnificent scenes of the South burning, to the huge landscapes, the not-so-repressed sexuality and the violence – not, I hope, to the lop-sided, demeaning, sado-masochistic relationship between Rhett and Scarlett.

Much later, after the war, when Scarlett, a brand new widow, is feeling guilty because her husband of convenience was killed defending her honour, Rhett – his timing immaculate as ever – asks her to marry him, and again forces a kiss upon her. This time she has been drinking brandy and responds to his kisses. 'I want you to faint,' he says. 'That's what you were meant for. None of the fools you've ever known have kissed you like this, have they?'

We know from the novel that they haven't: 'He was kissing her now and his mustache tickled her mouth, kissing her with slow, hot lips that were leisurely as though he had the whole night before him.' Her husband Charles had never kissed her like this. 'Never had the kisses of the Tarleton and Cavert boys made her go hot and cold and shaky like this. He bent her body backward and his lips traveled down her throat.'

She doesn't faint; she returns the kiss. The shot, carefully angled, commingles the Phallic Throat and the female version of the Thrusting Arm, her arm stretching up around his neck conveying the thrust of the action. It is very sexy. But when he asks her to marry him, she tells him she doesn't believe in marriage. He tells her what she needs is a real man, him. He forces another kiss; she squeals, and convinced, accepts the proposal of marriage. As he is leaving, she asks him if he isn't going to kiss her goodbye.

'Don't you think you've had enough kissing for one afternoon?' says Mr Know-it-all.

Gone With the Wind, the story of the beautiful and mercenary Scarlett's attempts to survive the Civil War and restore the family plantation Tara to its previous grandeur, tells of her love for two men, Ashley and Rhett. Clark Gable and Vivien Leigh's *Gone With the Wind* was not just a tamer version of Margaret Mitchell's romantic historical novel, it was also reslanted to make Scarlett narrower and her comeuppance plainer. Scarlett became another in a long line of Hollywood vamps, and got what Hollywood thought bad women deserved. Margaret Mitchell's Scarlett is a more complicated character, whose motives are of many shades of grey. Even in Technicolor, however, movies tended morally to be black and white. Reined in by the increasingly powerful Hays doctrine of bowdlerized community standards, the movies were lagging behind theatre and the novel in the treatment of controversial issues, and not just because of the time it took to adapt them.

Published in 1936, three years before the movie, Margaret Mitchell's book became an unprecedented bestseller, selling millions of copies. Its mixture of daring and traditional morals made the novel a commercial success. This also commended it to Hollywood producers, but not to the enforcers of the Code. As expected, a civil war ensued between the studio and the censors, with battles fought during each stage of the script and skirmishes even during the filming.

In the novel Rhett Butler comes home drunk one night and rapes his wife Scarlett:

He was like death, carrying her away in arms that hurt. She screamed, stifled against him, and he stopped suddenly on the landing and, turning her swiftly in his arms, bent over and kissed her with a savagery and a completeness that wiped out everything from her mind but the dark into which she was sinking and the lips on hers. He was shaking, as though he stood in a strong wind, and his lips, traveling from her mouth downward to where the wrapper had fallen from her body, fell on her soft flesh. He was muttering things she did not hear, his lips were evoking feelings never felt before.

Suddenly she had a wild thrill such as she had never known: joy, fear, madness, excitement, surrender.

Reveling in the fact that he was 'bullying and breaking her', Scarlett expresses a luxuriant sexual masochism that was once thought womanly. The union spoken of is of his lips on hers, but the mouths here become a euphemism. Later, her lips tremble beneath his. In the romantic novel, the kiss as a metaphor for orgasm was nothing new. Even the ultradiscreet Henry James had used it, in *Portrait of a Lady*. But no one could write in this genre better than Margaret Mitchell.

She awoke the next morning, he was gone and she remembered the glorious night when he had carried her up the stairs and then humbled her, hurt her, used her brutally through a wild mad night and she had gloried in it.

She had said no, but it turned out she really meant yes.

As the book's sales showed, very few readers of the day were appalled by what the Hollywood censor would refer to as 'the husbandly rape'. It had made Scarlett feel closer to Rhett. But the censor was worried. Couldn't some 'unexpected tenderness' on his part achieve the same thing? he asked.

The studio fought unusually hard, trading other *verboten*

scenes – of childbirth and brothels – in an attempt to gain leeway here. The Code's administrator recommended that Rhett Butler 'take [Scarlett] in his arms, kiss her, and then gently start with her toward the bedroom. It is our thought that you should not go so far as to throw her on the bed.' Rhett Butler 'should think more of his wife'. The censor would still exercise control, but the studio had won.

The man from the Code's office who was on the set for the filming of the rape scene stressed that Scarlett should not struggle against being carried away. Was this in hopes that no one would notice it was rape, or because more violence was thought to be more arousing? 'There should be no cries from Scarlett,' was the Code's recommendation. There weren't, although it is clear she does not want to be carried up the staircase. After a not-so-lingering fade-out on the staircase, suddenly it is morning.

To the audience of the time, a fade-out signalled sexual intercourse. It was a sexier end to the staircase scene than a cut would have been. Naturally, the Code men had wanted the cut. But they lost that round. We know only from the short fade-out and from the morning-after scene that Rhett and Scarlett have had sex. The 'rape' has been prettied up and we no longer know that he 'humbled her, hurt her, used her brutally . . . and she had gloried in it'. Instead, each of us can foist our own sexual fantasy on the scene. Gone, too, are the book's passionate kisses. The one kiss happens downstairs; the rape, unseen, upstairs. In the movie, in fact, it is not rape, it is very insistent seduction. An obviously sexually fulfilled Scarlett luxuriates contentedly alone in bed in the morning.

Gone With the Wind is perhaps the most famous rendition of the Hollywood conviction that when she said no, she meant yes. One of the most blatantly formulaic of these scenes occurs in the TNT stalwart *Gaiety George*. The hero, a vaude-ville entrepreneur, demands: 'Will you marry me or will you not? Answer me, woman.'

Her answer is 'no, no, no.' She falls into his arms. They kiss. The next scene is wedding bells.

Nice girls, we know, weren't supposed to want sex. Over-ruling them, even overpowering them, was seen as a way out of the dilemma. As it didn't then offend anyone, it worked in the movies, despite the troubles it caused in real life. Fred Astaire turned this song and dance into a parable in the kiss scene in *Top Hat*. 'When a clumsy cloud from here meets a fluffy little cloud from there,' he tells Ginger Rogers, 'he billows towards her. She scurries away, and he scuds right up to her. She cries a little, and there you have your shower. He comforts her. They spark. That's the lightning. They kiss. Thunder!'

Two decades after *Gone With the Wind*, in 1959, in *The Journey* Yul Brynner proves the same point to Deborah Kerr. Brynner plays a Russian officer in occupied Hungary who loves his horse and is in love with Deborah Kerr. To him, her allure is in her breeding. He comments on the centuries it has taken to develop that wan skin, that hair, those manicured hands. The kiss, when it finally comes, is another of those terrible ones in which the woman is forced and then likes it – reinforcing the ideology of date rape and marital rape. Ironically, it is Brynner who is sexy; in this movie, Kerr only exudes class.

Alas, in the future we would see many replays of the forced-kiss love scene, which we had been seeing since the days of the silents. In his tremendously successful *The Sheik* (1921) and *Son of the Sheik* (1925), Rudolph Valentino swooped out of the desert to carry women off, but in the end they were glad of it, so no harm done. Unlike the vamp, the predatory male was much admired. The *homme fatal*, we were to admire. He could seduce women in thrillingly unlikely ways, 'taking them' forcefully (or by force) into his arms, or bed, where they were happy and would perhaps even live happily ever after.

In the 1973 Western *High Plains Drifter,* the embittered hero Clint Eastwood rapes two women who like it. One, the town whore, fights even unto penetration – but then succumbs to his charms. The local respectable madonna – who also happens to be the only person of conscience in a town that once betrayed him – responds as soon as he knocks the knife out of her hand, throws her struggling on to the bed and kisses her deeply. The morning after shows her still languorously abed and very well disposed toward the rapist. Exactly like Scarlett.

Ingrid Bergman, in *For Whom the Bell Tolls* (1943), the movie version of the Hemingway novel, had to ask Gary Cooper for instruction. 'I don't know how to kiss, or I would kiss you. Where do the noses go?' But at least she thought she might like to take the initiative.

A year later in *To Have and Have Not* – her first kiss in her first movie – Lauren Bacall sits down uninvited on Humphrey Bogart's lap, taunts him with a few insults, leans forward, and kisses him.

'What'd you do that for?' Bogie asks.

'Wondering whether I'd like it.' Then she kisses him again.

As she leaves the room, Bogie has that stunned, kissed look. The kiss does not move the audience; it is her audacity and his reaction which does. This reversal, possible because the hero is such a tough guy, nonetheless made the studio nervous. Instead of ending the scene with the kiss, at the door as she is leaving Bacall makes a little speech that includes the famous line, 'If you want me, just whistle.'

The words enable Bogie to recover quickly from his

swoon. She has not only given over her power, she has given him a new power. When the door shuts behind her, Bogie tries out his whistle. The sound is of course the two-syllable wolf whistle.

There is another difference between Gable kissing Leigh, or any other woman, and the kisses Bacall foists on Bogie. Bogie does not initiate them but he certainly does not resist them. He is already sexually awake. It is women, remember, who are the sleeping beauties of storyland.

In *Casablanca*, at Rick's Café Americain, the pianist begins to play the song, 'You Must Remember This'. Rick (Humphrey Bogart) who has banned the song from his premises because it reminds him of his love affair with Ilsa, rushes over to upbraid the pianist, and sees her (Bergman). The moment is electric. Soon we hear her saying, 'Kiss me. Kiss me as if it were the last time.'

He doesn't. *They* do. They kiss as equals, she leaning forward to kiss him, he to kiss her.

During the kiss, though, she accidentally knocks over her brandy glass, which shatters, telling us symbolically that something has been broken in her life. When she and Rick were lovers in war-torn Paris, Ilsa had thought her husband, a Resistance leader, dead. Now she knows him to be alive. The kiss imperils Ilsa's honour. Rick's is not really tarnished. By the double standard, his sleeping with another man's wife is not particularly wrong; but her morality is shattered. The equality between them vanishes. So much for all the liberated ideology that has been read into this movie.

At the end comes the scene in which she says yes, but is told she means no. With the Germans closing in, Rick uses his black-market connections to buy two seats on the last plane out of Casablanca, presumably for himself and Bergman. At the airport at the last minute, for the greater good, he insists she depart with her husband. The world needs him, and therefore her own hopes must be sacrificed. This is the famous non-kiss scene.

What is usually viewed as the victory of Rick's sense of decency over desire, his patriotism and honour transcending 'the hots', has always seemed to me insufferable. How dare he decide for her. When I saw it the first time as a student, I resented his choosing for the little woman and saddling her with an unhappy marriage for, at the very least, the duration. When I saw it again recently, twenty years later, on a plane in inglorious Turner-tinted colour, I still resented it. But until that false moment of imposed renunciation – his manful maturity, her infantilization – *Casablanca*'s honest inter-mingling of mutually reined lust is transfixing.

In *You Must Remember This,* his literary spoof of the movie *Casablanca*, Robert Coover retells the story with a contemporary sensibility, putting in the lurid moments hinted at but never shown on the screen. Published nearly half a century after the movie first appeared, Coover's superbly vulgar story is told in lip movements.

Rick, finding Ilsa in his apartment ('I told you this morning you'd come round,'), is seen 'curling his lips as if to advertise his appetite for punishment'. Then he asks if she has come for the letters of transit, 'his upper lip swelling with bitterness and hurt'. 'As long as I have those letters, I'll never be lonely.' A sardonic smile 'plays on his lips'.

She 'presses her lips together', preparing to say, 'We luffed each other once.' 'Her lower lip pushed forward as though bruised,' she offers him the truth.

'I wouldn't believe you no matter what you told me,' he says.

'Her lips are drawn back' in hurt retreat. When he tells her to shoot him if she wants the letters of transit, she is taken aback, 'her lips swollen and parted'.

But instead of the kiss we are now primed for, he makes the Freudian equation and goes straight to her breast, eager 'to kiss it or eat it: he seems ravenously hungry'. They fall to the floor, both groping, gripping, and he heaves his penis upward: '"Oh Gott" she screams, her back arching, mouth agape as though to commence "La Marseillaise".'

There is much, much more before he says, 'Jesus, I've been saving that one for a goddamn year and a half . . . !'

'It was the best fokk I effer haff.' She kisses his ear.

Instead of the brandy glass shattering, Ilsa drinks Grand Marnier while straddling the bidet, pouring what's left over his penis to facilitate a blow job, which commences when 'she puckers her lips and kisses the tip'.

During this fellatio, he remembers their idyll in Paris – the blow job she gave him in a movie theatre during a newsreel of that month's Nazi conquests of Europe, and the one that nearly caused him to wreck his car in the Bois de Bologne. Then, it is her turn, and as he begins the kiss he knows she really wants, Rick again remembers Paris – that magical first time she asked him for cunnilingus, 'Kiss me, Richard, here. My other mouth wants to luff you, too.'

Rick is not sure he wants to: 'He had never tasted one of those things before. Other women had sucked him off, of course . . . but reciprocation, sucking back – well, that always struck him as vaguely queer.' But he forced himself in Paris, and was converted. So now 'he plunges his face deep into Ilsa's ambrosial pudding'.

Comical nitty-gritty replaces the movie's gritty sentimentalism. The symbolic kiss of the beginning of the movie and the famous non-kiss at the end of it when Rick nobly sends Ilsa off with her husband are transformed to the bumping and grinding of coitus and the 'kisses' of oral sex. The magic of their affair in Paris is unmasked; it is based not in timeless romance, not in the meetings of souls, but in the here and now, in the fingerings and fuckings of the body, in the kisses of the nether regions, in the physicality of sex.

Like so many other movies – like every movie, really – *Casablanca* omits to mention that.

The kiss on the beach between Deborah Kerr and Burt Lancaster in *From Here to Eternity* is the third sexiest kiss in the Gallup pantheon. They lie in the Hawaiian surf and kiss ravenously for a long time. It is hard to think of another kiss scene, at least before a couple of decades had passed, which had so visceral an impact.

The kiss starts in the deep surf. To avoid drowning in anything but passion, they run on to the edge of the beach, and resume kissing. One more than senses the presence of the beast with two backs, although even at the climax of the scene they are touching only above the waist and both are wearing swimsuits. Yet this kiss in the spume of the crashing waves not only signifies mutual passionate intimacy and sexual pleasure, it represents orgasm.

The sheer physicality of the scene is tremendous, the power of the ocean expressive of the strength of their mutual desire which the dialogue undercuts.

The movie, much more brazen visually than the book, is coyer verbally. 'Nobody ever kissed me the way you do,' Kerr sighs after the scene on the beach. In the book, what she says is 'Nobody ever loved me like you love me.'

'Nobody?' he asks, as the scene begins to turn nasty—his insecurity and jealousy suddenly transformed into an indictment of her morals. 'Nobody? Out of all the many men you've been loved by?' In the movie, for propriety's sake, he says 'kissed by.' And then he asks her to estimate how many men there have been.

Hiding her hurt with a false bravado, she says she can't possibly estimate without an adding machine.

In the book, the conversation takes place in bed in a hotel room after they have made love and is a foil for a three-page diatribe about her hysterectomy, and how it has made sex meaningless (you can't have babies). So detailed is the medical stuff, you can practically see the author copying it out of the medical encyclopedia. The hotel, we learn in passing, has an ocean view – but no one is looking at the ocean.

There are two relevant beach scenes in the book, but they are minor. The author prefers beds for sex. They swim nude, but nothing is quite right, and there is no kiss. Yet one can see how the scriptwriter transformed the sentences that follow into the movie's sex-in-the-surf scene.

First we hear of the secret little beach out near the Blowhole. Riding past he had imagined that 'it would be such a wonderful place for a man to take a woman'. The beach seems about to live up to his fantasy of expectation: 'It was all there, the full moon, the small mild surf showing white, the pale sands of the tiny beach set down among the rocks and glowing weirdly in the moonlight, the low wind surfing through the kiawe trees across the highway, and he had bought a bottle and there was a thermos of coffee and the sandwiches she had brought, and even blankets. It was really all there and very fine.'

Reality impinges when she slips climbing down the rocks, skinning her arm, and tears her dress, one of her best ones. Undaunted, 'They had waded, nude, out into the water, hand in hand, making, he remembered, a fine picture in the moonlight with the water that seemed to run uphill from the beach breathing heavily around their knees. She had gotten chilled and had to go back and wrap up in a blanket. It was then he had given up altogether, deciding it had been a damn fool thing, *his* mistake.'

Much later in the book there is another beach scene with

a kiss, but not one that takes the breath away. And a nice warm bed looms: 'There was nobody around the patio and he kissed her then, standing out on the beach still, the bad of a while ago all gone now, finding it now just as he had thought so long about it being, before they went up to the nice room, the fine room, that was on the second floor.'

The adultery between the Captain's wife and Sergeant Warden broke all the rules of the Code, which forbade any condoning of adultery. The battle for Code approval of *From Here to Eternity* took six months. James Jones's sensational novel contained so much potentially censorable material that many in the movie business were sure it would never be released. But the balance of power had shifted. By now it was tacitly understood that adultery might be shown and enjoyed so long as the miscreants suffered in some way.

The Code's director was demanding 'a strong voice for morality by which their immoral relationship can be denounced'. The script was rewritten to stress the Captain's infidelity and cruelty, as a mitigating circumstance of the wife's behaviour. Jones's novel had been utterly uncompromising; the movie didn't so much bow as wave off-handedly at convention. One line, in which the Captain's wife regrets her adultery, was added to the parting scene. Lip service.

Some kisses remain taboo. The only Hollywood leading ladies never to have kissed their leading men were Mae West and Anna May Wong. One theory is that Mae West exuded such physicality that actual contact would have been too much. Racism is definitely what kept the Chinese-American Anna May Wong unkissed. A kissing scene was shot in the British film *The Road to Dishonour* (1929), but was cut on the grounds that inter-racial love would offend the audience.

The first inter-racial kiss in the American movies must be the one played for laughs in Edison's *What Happened in the*

Tunnel? (1903), in which two women – a white lady and her black maid – are on a train which goes through a tunnel. In the dark of the tunnel, a white man tries to steal a kiss from the white woman and mistakenly kisses the black one. It ends with the man wiping his face with a handkerchief and the women laughing together at him. A fool he is, but only because the audience shares the implied racist sentiments. In *Guess Who's Coming to Dinner* (1967), instead of a direct shot, you see the black man and white woman kissing briefly only in the mirror – and even so, when the movie first appeared, the scene was controversial.

In the movie industry, as in the rest of American society, blacks are constructed as a problem issue. Ordinary romance, therefore, isn't what usually comes to the white director's mind, and the black director's agenda may be urgent; he skips kissing and has his characters jump into bed. There are exceptions, of course, but on the whole, Hollywood is still not eager for a black-and-white *When Harry Met Sally*.

Part of the shockingness of *Sunday Bloody Sunday* (1971) was that it refused to be deviant. The story concerned a bisexual male designer, played by Murray Head, who alternated between his two lovers, a doctor (Peter Finch) and an executive (Glenda Jackson). There was no sex scene in the Penelope Gilliatt novel, but the film's director John Schlesinger insisted the two men kiss. Head arrives at Finch's house and kisses him hello. The kiss between the two male stars is made to seem as though it happened everyday. Schlesinger says, 'I wanted them to embrace and kiss quite passionately as lovers but not to make a big deal of it. It should happen as though it happened every time they met. It was not, here are these twilight people driven to each other with these terrible appetites which somehow they slake with their impure lips. It was, Hi honey, what's for lunch? or what's for dinner?' Thirty years later, in the comedy *French Twist/*

Gazon Maudit, which also features a triangle, the lesbian relationship is also taken for granted by the end of the film.

In *My Beautiful Laundrette* (1985), a white man and a black man kiss beneath a street lamp, and in the laundrette. One dribbles champagne from his mouth into the other's. Their kisses, inter-racial and homosexual, broke two taboos. The film, though widely distributed, had been made by an independent company. With a smaller budget to recoup, it could take more chances than *Philadelphia* would feel able to nearly a decade later. The film that broke the AIDS barrier is happy to show men holding each other, dancing, open about gay relationships, but the moment that Tom Hanks's mouth is about to meet Antonio Banderas's the back of a head moves in to eclipse the scene. To the mass audience, this is forbidden territory.

In an age of more innocence and less sexual fear than ours, *The Age of Innocence* would never have attracted the interest of a director like Martin Scorsese. Leaving the mean streets of the twentieth-century urban jungle and the dilemma of AIDS, he takes us into the plush interiors of Edith Wharton's novel of New York in the 1870s. Surprisingly, in this elegant, repressive milieu, Scorsese is no raging bull in a china shop. Under his direction, Daniel Day Lewis and Michelle Pfeiffer, lovers sundered by upper-class social codes as ruthless as the Mafia's, have little opportunity, but make the most of it. In the movie's set piece, Day Lewis kisses the back of Pfeiffer's gloved hand. Constrained by convention from going further, they imbue their socially safe sex with intensity and desire. The kiss also becomes a metaphor for safe sex.

The spectre of AIDS has created a new romantic consciousness, born of caution. People get to know each other now before jumping into bed. They take things slowly. The increasingly frequent theme of sexual repression in current movies and the advent of respectable soft porn for women, too, in anthologies like *Slow Hand*, are reflections of this change in our sexual ideology. Films like *Howard's End* and *The Age of Innocence* which peruse eras noted for their repression depict a restrained, indeed, a reined-in sexuality.

In *Four Weddings and a Funeral*, the reserved British hero and the forward American heroine meet at a wedding. At the first opportunity she invites him to her hotel room, but he finds words to delay the first kiss. To get things going, when finally he (Hugh Grant) does follow her (Andie McDowell) into the room, she sits on the edge of the bed grasping the long phallic bedpost, and talks about kissing: 'I noticed the bride and groom didn't kiss in the church which is kind of strange. Where I come from kissing's very big.'

It is big in England too. Just slower to come to the fore. More teasing discussion and they kiss. Their edgy inarticulate banter brings to mind the very different, flowery discussion of kissing almost exactly a hundred years earlier in *Cyrano de Bergerac*:

> A kiss, when all is said, what can it be?
> An oath that makes one closer than before;
> A promise more precise; the sealing of
> Confessions that before were barely breathed;
> A rosy letter in the alphabet of love.

Cyrano too inhabited an over-mannered world, one frightened of intimacy and sex and forced therefore to delay it.

The director Anthony Minghella finds kisses hard to film, he says, because they exclude the audience and because there has been so much kissing in movies that it is hard to make a kiss carry meaning. 'If there are any physical transactions,' he says, 'you make them strange in some way in order to point up their meaning.' In what is regarded as one of the 1990s' most romantic movies, *Truly Madly Deeply*, which he wrote as well as directed, Juliet Stevenson is grieving so hard for dead partner Alan Rickman that he comes back to her. Their kiss, a long kiss, ends with an audible smack, and the words, 'Your lips are a bit cold.'

This is not so much magic realism as magic necrophilia, but we are to take it as quite wholesome. Loving necrophiliacs who miss their husbands are, apparently, completely socially acceptable.

THE JUDGEMENTS OF PARIS

On April Fool's Day 1950, the *Life* magazine photographer snapped the picture of the two lovers kissing in the street. Later, that click of the shutter would be recognized as a kind of cultural freeze-frame, a defining moment in the popular iconography of love. Seemingly oblivious to the bustle of Paris, to onlookers, to whatever else is going on around them, the lovers sense only each other. A thick scarf loosely caresses his neck which is taut with intensity as he leans down to her upturned face. Every muscle of her body seems to be straining towards him.

Few know it by name, but millions of people have seen a reproduction of the photograph somewhere. In the last decade or so, a few million of them have pinned it, postcard- or poster-sized, on to their walls. *The Kiss at City Hall* (*Le Baiser à l'Hôtel de Ville*), Robert Doisneau's most famous photograph, has come to symbolize the romance of Paris. That the photo is so often reproduced it has become a cliché hardly matters. Indeed, it may help. Part of the reason for Rodin's pervasive reputation is that there are a number of copies of his sculpture *The Kiss*, each functioning as an advertisement. Doisneau's photograph has now probably replaced Rodin's sculpture as the most famous representation of the erotic kiss in the world.

That students at universities around the world pin up this Doisneau picture with the dominant man reaching down to the little woman shows that our idea of romance is as firmly stuck in the past as the poster is stuck on the walls. In the Rodin, too, the woman's neck is upstretched. Is this just an instance of anatomy being destiny – the woman, being smaller, reaches up? Or is there something about the man bending down to bestow the kiss on the woman, something about her being kissed, which appealed to the male sculptor, the male photographer and to the multitude?

Somehow, it took thirty-eight years for Jean-Louis and Denise Lavergne to come upon the photograph but when they saw it on the cover of the French weekly television magazine *Telerama* in 1988 they thought they recognized themselves. They had been just there in the rue de Rivoli on 1 April, 1950, the day the photograph was taken, and had a diary to prove it. Madame Lavergne still had the skirt and jacket she wore that day, and Monsieur recognized the scarf he was wearing, a blue one his sister had given him for Christmas. They contacted Doisneau to say that they were the couple in the photograph. Doisneau, they say, was charming and told them, 'You are now in my family.' He was making five-figure amounts each year from the posters; he offered them nothing. Nor did they want anything. At first.

They were delighted to be part of the history of romance. They were filmed for a TV documentary about Doisneau's work, but when the footage of them wound up on the cutting-room floor they were, they said, appalled that the most romantic moment of their life had been cut from under their feet. They decided to go to court to prove that they were the couple of legend and reclaim the stolen kiss. Under a 1985 French privacy law, they claimed that their image had been stolen from them by the photographer and demanded many francs in damages.

Whereupon an actress named Françoise Bornet emerged from the negatives of time saying that she and her then lover were the people in the photograph. They had been paid a small amount to pose for the picture. Now she was suing for more, and a percentage of future proceeds. The man she had posed with wanted no part of the action.

Much was at stake in the case: the romantic heritage of the Lavergnes; the faith of the millions of people who believed the photo to be a snatched moment of truth; the livelihood of photographers who would have to be certain to get releases signed whenever they took a photograph, whether in the midst of a bombardment or a bar.

The agency that handled Doisneau's photos produced what they said were the contact sheets of the original shoot, which showed that a few versions of the photo had been taken – in a café, on the street. Like the famous American war photo of the raising of the flag on Iwo Jima, this document of love had been posed.

It was the judgement of the court of Paris that the Lavergnes were not the couple in the photograph. The kiss had not been stolen from them; it had been bought from the paid models.

The belief that the icon was candid love captured was proved to be an illusion. It was verisimilitude, the appearance of truth, artistic illusion, to which we responded, and continue to respond. But the publicity of the law case made even more people aware of the photograph. There is no reason to think those posters will be pulled down.

Of all the arts, photography especially brings home the

fact that we live in a culture of simulacra, copies. In the icons by Rodin and Doisneau, the sense of the original has been lost in a way that is still not the rule in art, a way that plunges the sculpture and the photograph into what the French writer Baudrillard has called the world of the hyper-real, the hyper-reality of simulacra. The big Rodin marble *Kiss* at the Tate in London seems to the viewer to be the real thing. But what, then, of the one at the Rodin Museum in Paris, and the others elsewhere? To many more people than have actually seen the sculpture, the real Rodin *Kiss* is a flat picture on a computer screen or in a book. Or is the real *Kiss* the one the most people have put their lips to – the British postage stamp of 1995? For the stamp, though, the image was cropped; nothing is left below the waist. Because familiarity breeds contempt, over-replication has transformed Rodin's *Kiss* for some people into bad art, kitsch. Rodin had his doubts about it too.

As workmen wheeled the big, marble sculpture out of the studio and through the courtyard, Rodin examined it in the daylight, his grey-blue eyes roaming over the contours of the two naked figures embracing, their mouths joined in a kiss. It was only a few days to the opening of the Paris Salon of 1898, where this larger-than-life-sized *Kiss* (*Le Baiser*) was to be shown along with 7,000 other works of art. Rodin gazed up at the polished white marble and made his judgement: 'I was not dissatisfied with the strength of my marble. As it went by, however, I had the sensation that it was a little flabby.'

Along with *The Kiss* Rodin was exhibiting *Balzac*, an undignified portrait of the great man which Rodin believed to be the best thing he had ever done. However, when Monsieur le Président came to view the Salon, he congratulated Rodin on *The Kiss* and just walked on without seeming to notice the controversial *Balzac*. It would have to fight hard for its place in the canon but *The Kiss* now had the imprimatur of the President of the Republic.

Partly because it was not *Balzac*, partly because for a government commission it was cutting-edge risqué, partly because so many think love is grand, *The Kiss,* which is not Rodin's most erotic sculpture and is far from his best, became a twentieth-century cultural icon. Yet Western culture's most famous sculptural kiss is also one of the most misunderstood. *The Kiss* has shocked or confused or pleased a great many people, many of whom wrongly assess the intention and the meaning of the sculpture, and are unaware that Rodin did almost none of the carving himself. Do these fused marble mouths sum up all human desire? Is Rodin's the kiss of kisses?

The painter Benjamin Constant certainly thought so. 'What a masterpiece!' he said in *Le Figaro* soon after the Salon. 'Never before has marble seemed so alive. Never has a kiss joined two people in so beautiful and sculptural a caress. This is the expression of an artist's in-most heart.'

But was it? 'No doubt the entwinement in *The Kiss* is pretty enough, but it meant nothing to me,' Rodin confessed. 'The theme is treated in the academic tradition.' It was bread-and-butter work.

Its admirers see the work as a balancing act between idealized bodies and realistic sexiness: 'Its power', says a guide to the Tate, where the sculpture is one of the biggest draws, 'derives from its beautifully judged balance between a high degree of idealization in the depiction of the bodies of the couple and the equally high degree of eroticism.'

It is in fact more a balancing act between lust and lucre. The 'poet of the flesh, the sculptor of voluptuousness' reined himself in to make this early public commission acceptable. The sculpture became a money-spinner as orders for copies came in. Big ones, small ones, none of them made by Rodin.

He did model the clay original, or most of it. Rodin had many assistants. He had first created the two entwined figures of *The Kiss* as a bas-relief attached to the *Gates of Hell*, a huge portal adorned with dozens of sculpted figures he had been working on for years. In 1882 he completed *The Kiss* as a half-life-sized free-standing clay sculpture in its own right. Because clay cracks if it is not kept wet, all Rodin's sculptures had to be transferred into more permanent media, and it was cast into bronze. Specialists did the work. Rodin preferred bronze and plaster to marble because casts retained the rough patina of the original clay which gave the sculpture life. Most rich collectors, however, preferred polished white marble to rough bronze. So did the arbiters of public taste. To please them Rodin hired *praticiens* to do the carving and gave each marble a few finishing touches, often carving little more than his signature.

When in 1887 the French government supplied a block of Italian marble and commissioned Rodin to produce a larger-than-life *Kiss*, he hired the marble specialist Jean Turcan to carve it. This is the one that was finally completed and exhibited in the Salon of 1898, and is now in the Rodin Museum in Paris.

In the years when he was modelling *The Kiss*, Rodin walked around with a copy of Dante's *Divine Comedy* crammed into his back pocket, and read over and over the famous lines: 'One day, to our delight, we read of Lancelot, how love constrained him . . . When we read how that fond smile was kissed by such a lover, trembling, he kissed my trembling mouth. We read no more that day.' This reluctant moment is the one that Rodin has depicted. In the sculpture the book can just be made out, still clutched in the surprised Paolo's left hand.

Rodin was not the first artist for whom Dante's book provided a good classical justification for modelling naked figures in erotic poses; and who is to say that Dante himself did not in choosing the story of Paolo and Francesca use a supposedly worthy subject for the same purpose? Poets are an earthy lot. Scholars, on the other hand, will believe anything of poets; even that they love God more than women. At the very least, Rodin subverted the Christian Dante's meaning. At the very worst, he played the same confidence trick that Dante had.

Finding Dante was a wonderful boon to Rodin, staving off the charges of immorality which were always being levelled at him. Rodin was obsessed with bodies. His figures obey not the laws of God but the laws of the flesh. It is the earthy realism of Dante rather than his Christian faith that appealed to Rodin. For him, works needed no titles, they formed their own bodies; but names were necessary for catalogues and sales. Using literary antecedents lent a legitimacy to his sexual themes which, had they not had such high-falutin cultural titles, might have been pronounced vulgar, the erotic deemed to have crossed the line of propriety into the pornographic.

It was said that the greatest sculptor of the century had his head pointed in the direction opposite the clouds, but Rodin made no apologies. Walking one evening in his garden with the visiting English painter William Rothenstein, Rodin gazed at the Seine and the distant panorama of Paris, and said: 'People say I think too much about women.'

'I was going to answer with conventional sympathy – but how absurd!' recalls Rothenstein, 'when Rodin, after a moment's reflection, added – "yet, after all, what is there more important to think about?"'

Rodin once told his friend Judith Cladel that 'Lovers are besotted idiots, they can never keep their heads.' It is droll that the attempt to keep one's head is what *The Kiss* is meant to depict. What is generally regarded as a moment of great passion is actually the moment *before* Reason falls to Passion. The male figure sits upright, withholding, holding back. This restraint is not characteristic of Rodin's work. As Marie Laurent, a former curator of the Rodin Museum in Paris, has said, it is his most famous and his least typical. The Rodin Museum is full of erotic sculptures that hold nothing back.

In 1900, during the Exposition Universelle, Rodin enterprisingly installed his own huge exhibition of no fewer than 165 sculptures, plus a room of drawings and the towering *Gates of Hell*. It is still not customary for a sculptor to stage his own retrospective, and many visitors thought it part of the official exposition: that Rodin was being honoured, when actually he was blowing his own horn.

Admission to Exposition Rodin cost one franc during the week, five francs on Fridays. On Sundays, when there was no charge, the crowds were gargantuan. Rodin was often there, talking to visitors, and personally showed a great many, including Oscar Wilde, around the hall. Wilde, who was ostracized by many after his term in gaol, greatly admired what he called Rodin's 'dreams in marble'. The phrase comes from the Baudelaire poem which is carved into the base of *The Kiss*. Despite the millions of one francs paid to see the show, at its conclusion Rodin had serious debts. So, hallelujahs greeted the order from Copenhagen, from the Danish brewer and collector Carl Jacobsen, for several sculptures and a duplicate of the marble *The Kiss*.

A week later came another order, from the American collector Edward Perry Warren. A classical scholar from an old Bostonian family, Warren, who was homosexual, lived abroad in England. America's loss would become London's gain. Warren's *Kiss*, now on permanent display at the Tate, is slightly larger than the French one, but otherwise virtually identical, except for the penis. The contract stipulated that 'the genital organ of the man is to be represented in its entirety.' The Paris marble has a slight depression where there should be a bulge. This castration, for reasons of propriety, must have been a source of great hilarity at the Rodin *atelier*. 'If I could have,' Rodin said, 'I would have shown the male member.'

There is a fault in the Paris marble; a patch at the back is visible. Warren was persuaded to pay three times the usual rate so that better marble could be obtained for the statue. Since Turcan had died, Warren's *Kiss* was carved by another *practicien*, Rigaud.

In 1914 Warren arranged to have the four-ton *Kiss* exhibited in the Town Hall at Lewes, and hoped the English town would keep his Rodin indefinitely. But many people in Lewes thought the statue immoral. Worried lest it corrupt soldiers attending concerts at the town hall, the council draped it in black. It was returned to him in 1917, and remained out of the way in Warren's carriage house until his death in 1928. Warren had tried to give it to Boston. His heirs tried to sell it to Kansas City. Later, an inopportune offer from the American art collector Huntington Hartford was refused by the daughter of Warren's heir. She wanted the sculpture to stay in Britain and did not even go to meet Hartford at the Savoy: 'Being just after the war, I did not have anything suitable to wear.' Eventually *The Kiss* was purchased by the Tate. The Danish *Kiss* is now in the Carlsberg Glyptotek in Copenhagen. A fourth was produced after Rodin's death, for the Rodin Museum in Philadelphia.

On an April day almost exactly a hundred years after the 1898 Salon, as I stood looking at the Paris *Kiss,* an American mother and daughter arrived. The daughter gazed boldly, the mother very shyly. 'I guess I'm just a prude,' she said, backing away. It was hard to imagine how anyone who had ever seen a love scene in a movie could be embarrassed. Then I realized movies aren't three-dimensional and you don't stand close enough to touch.

The best answer to those who are still shocked by *The Kiss* is still that made by Rodin's friend Besnard. Wondering what the fuss was all about in 1898 he said, 'But surely you can see it's merely two models posing? Those lovers have never slept together, and haven't the slightest wish to!' More than half a century later Libero Nadonne, who had been the male model for the sculpture revealed that actually he wouldn't have minded, but Rodin and Carmen, the female model, had already embarked on an affair.

Brancusi referred derisively to work like Rodin's as 'beef-steak'. Rodin was known for leaving a statue half-hewn, Constantin Brancusi (1867–1957) went further. His *Kiss* remains, above all, a rectangular block of stone. His lovers, eye to eye, lip to lip, arms encircling each other, are carved into the sculptural landscape, not carved out of it. Theirs is an embrace of the modern world.

Brancusi arrived in Paris from Romania practically penni-less and worked as a dishwasher until Paris judged he was a sculptor. From 1907 onwards, he carved several very similar versions of his *Kiss*. In none of them do we sense the lust of humankind. His is a representation of the *idea*, not the emo-tion of a kiss. It is an image of reciprocity and commingling, but, it does seem somewhat bereft of passion. Yet Brancusi truly believed in the power of the kiss as a unifying symbol of both erotic love and peace; he sensed the kiss continuum.

The first version of his *Kiss* was installed in Montparnasse Cemetery on the grave of Tatiana Rashewsky, whose suicide had been occasioned by an unhappy love affair. Her parents, who had commissioned it, were not enthralled with the sculpture, but Brancusi would not change it; he thought it very suitable for a martyr to love. Later versions commemor-ated spiritual love and world peace.

Unlike Rodin's, Brancusi's *Kiss* was not just bread-and-butter work. Yet the moiling and toiling of muscles gave Rodin's stone the greater vitality of the heart. Brancusi's simplified forms lost contact with the primal. Better taste than Rodin, but lesser passion. Brancusi's *Kiss* did not become an erotic icon.

Doisneau's photograph and Rodin's sculpture did. Both works originated in Paris, so the decisions about them and, by implication, about the nature of a kiss were made there. But the very first famous judgement of Paris had nothing whatever to do with the city. That story is told in the Iliad.

IN CONCLUSION

The King of Troy's handsome son Paris was asked to decide which of three goddesses was the most beautiful. And he was foolish enough to agree to do it. To bribe him, Minerva promised success in war, Juno wealth and power, but Venus offered the most beautiful mortal woman in the world. Perhaps because of the bribe or perhaps because it was true, Paris said Venus was the fairest of them all, earning the enmity of the other two goddesses.

Under the protection of the goddess of love he sailed to Greece, where he was received as the guest of the King of Sparta, Menelaus, and his wife the renowned beauty Helen. Before long, Paris persuaded his hostess to run off with him to Troy.

After ten years of war in which Paris was killed and Troy destroyed, Helen returned to Menelaus. As she boarded her husband's boat, the other Greeks gasped at the beauty of 'the face that launch'd a thousand ships'. Fighting a war over a woman had not seemed a good idea to some of them; now they could see the reason for it. Centuries later, men were still gasping at her beauty: 'Sweet Helen, make me immortal with a kiss!'

But did Helen think it was worth it? Sara Teasdale's *Helen of Troy* (1911) thought not:

> Though I know he loves me,
> Tonight my heart is sad;
> His kiss is not so wonderful
> As all the dreams I had.

For most of us, though, the reality is more luscious, more delicious than any reverie. The kiss *qua* kiss, as a thing in itself, is truly remarkable. It can make the body tingle and the genitalia glow. It can generate lust as well as whatever it is that we mean by love. Our arousal, however, Roger Scruton argues in *Sexual Desire*, is a response to an idea rather than to a sensation. You are responding to your idea of the other person, he says, rather than to the physicality of that person. Surely he is wrong, except in one sense: few of us go to bed more than once or twice with a body – either it becomes a person to us or we move on to another one.

But do we kiss people or do we kiss lips? Or are we really kissing something else altogether? Are the lips of the mouth an advertisement for the lips of the vagina? Are lips, which are the opening to the moist, mucoid, interior region of the mouth, merely stand-ins for the labia?

The contentious argument that the lips are an evolutionary billboard goes like this. A chimpanzee who wants to know if a female is willing to have sex has only to look at her genitalia, which become large and pink and highly conspicuous if she is in estrus, signalling that she is eager for coitus. Jane Goodall's field notes report: 'Flo arrives in camp early, accompanied by David Greybeard and Goliath. It is the second day of her full sexual swelling, and both males copulate with her before taking a single banana.' The swelling of Flo's genital area is so vividly pink that it can be seen from the trees and from nearly a kilometre away across a wide valley.

When humans stood upright and the rosy swollen labia were no longer easily visible, say proponents of the billboard view, nature found it necessary to provide the mimicry of lips. The zoologist Desmond Morris is a promulgator but not the originator of this idea that the labia are the forerunner of human lips. It is irrelevant, Morris says, that men have lips too. Many of his colleagues disagree with the whole idea. Human lips, they say, evolved as signals for feeding not fucking.

But even if nature did not make the equation, Madison Avenue and Hollywood certainly did. Marilyn Monroe's open-mouthed pout, which she herself parodied in the later films, is seen in all the best pornography. The most famous Marilyn photograph of all is the shot from the *Seven Year Itch* (1955) in which she is standing over a subway grating, the hot air coming from beneath blowing her skirt crotch high. Her lips and her legs are parted invitingly. She pretends to be entirely unaware of the effect she is having on a male bystander. The film critic John Russell Taylor thinks the picture is 'one of the most universally-known, instantly recognizable images in the whole of the twentieth century' and wonders why it is so effective. Because there she is, a living, breathing, available inflatable doll. The legs are already parted, receiving the heat. The lips, ready too, have a dual purpose; the same purpose they have in Andy Warhol's silk-screen repeated print of Marilyn. They are at once kissable and fuckable.

The use of the mouth for fellatio or cunnilingus is at the borderline of our subject. Both activities involve many of the same mouth movements used in kissing and may be used as preliminaries to coitus or as ends in themselves. Exactly like kissing. Oral sex, which has been called 'the genital kiss', is still illegal in some American states even if practised by the legally married. In England, in 1640, it was a suitable subject for poetry. These lines are from *A Rapture* by the Cavalier poet Thomas Carew:

> And, where the beauteous region doth divide
> Into two milky ways, my lips shall slide
> Down those smooth alleys, wearing as I go
> A tract for lovers on the printed snow;
> Thence climbing o'er the swelling Apennine
> Retire into thy grove of eglantine
> Where I will all those ravished sweets distill.

Three hundred years later, the sexologist Havelock Ellis reported in detail that cunnilingus was widely practised, and mentioned an unusual technique used by the indigenous people of the Caroline Islands: 'It is here customary for a man to place a piece of fish between the labia, while he stimulates the latter by his tongue and teeth until under stress of sexual excitement the woman urinates; this is regarded as an indication that the proper moment for intercourse has arrived. Such a practice rests physiologically on sound facts whatever may be thought of it from an aesthetic standpoint.'

Women writing about cunnilingus express none of the ambivalence that some men do. And lesbian writers in particular express ardour and pleasure. In *Art and Lies*, Jeannette Winterson hails 'the rosary I find between your legs'. The American poet Adrienne Rich speaks of the innocence and of the wisdom of the place her tongue has found. Her love poems speak too of lovers who do not merely reach deep, but touch deeply. In her story of a first love, 'Viyella', Susan

Griffin writes: 'I wanted her. Wanted to reach inside her, even as I ached to have her put her hands, her mouth in me.'

In Anais Nin's *Delta of Venus*, a young man feels the same ardour: 'Suddenly she opened the kimono, took his head between her hands, placed it on her sex for his mouth to feel. The tendrils of pubic hair touched his lips and maddened him.'

Luce Irigaray, the French feminist theorist, attracted a lot of bemused attention with her assertion that female sexuality is based in the self-kiss of the vagina's lips: 'A woman "touches herself" constantly without anyone being able to forbid her to do so, for her vulva is composed of two lips which embrace continually. Thus, within herself she is already two – but not divisible into ones – who stimulate each other.' In most English translations, where I have used the words 'her vulva', one sees 'her sex'. In French, *le sexe* is the word for vulva. My translation loses the *double entendre* but, I think, makes more sense. Even so, the notion that we go about all the time in a stimulated state of self-kiss seems dubious to me, but would surely be understood by the school of late twentieth-century male literary onanists that has burgeoned since Philip Roth made masturbation fashionable – or at least portrayable – in *Portnoy's Complaint*. The hero of Nicholson Baker's novel *The Fermata* asks what else there is in the world beside masturbation. With verbal onanism, he answers himself, 'Nothing'. The practice, which also appears in Baker's earlier novel *Vox,* has now spilled across the Atlantic into books by a stream of British novelists including Ian McEwan, Martin Amis, Julian Barnes and Will Self. I am making no judgement of them. To quote Swift: 'Why everyone as they like; as the good woman said when she kissed her cow.'

More dangerous is Camille Paglia who seems to misunderstand sex and reiterates the more bizarre aspects of the old Darwinian sex tooth and claw view. In *Sexual Personae* Paglia asserts that 'sexual intercourse, from kissing to penetration, consists of movements of barely controlled cruelty and consumption.' In fact, sexuality is about controlled movements leading to uncontrolled movements of sensuality and pleasure.

Reading or listening to Camille Paglia you suspect that this is a woman who finds words sexier than bodies. But who cares if she practises orgasm by monograph or monologue; to each her own.

The hero of Saul Bellow's novel, *Henderson, the Rain King,* like a large proportion of today's bourgeoisie, even the petty bourgeoisie, engaged in oral sex: When he can't reach his lover's lips, Henderson says, 'I plant my kisses further down.' !Kung lovers touch each other's genitalia but oral sex was, Nisa explained to the Harvard anthropologist, taboo: 'Women don't take men's genitals into their mouths.' Nor do men kiss women's genitals, 'because a woman's genitals could burn a man's mouth.' This is not a widely held view.

But in his book *The Mouth and Oral Sex* (1969) Paul Ableman's distaste is evident: 'One can imply, by performing oral/genital contact, that nothing about the loved one is offensive.' He suggests it can be 'a chivalrous challenge, the acceptance of which expresses some such sentiment as: "See how much I love you – if I am prepared to do this." Putting one's mouth to the genital regions, breaching the hygiene taboos and conventions of decency, is in fact a gesture of intimacy that transcends coitus itself.'

It must have been men like Ableman that Germaine Greer was talking about when she said on the television programme *Face to Face* that British men love blow jobs but hate to reciprocate. The interviewer Jeremy Isaacs said not at all: we both know the British Nijinsky of cunnilingus whose name was not revealed. In fact, according to the 1994 sociological survey *Sex in America*, both sexes vastly prefer receiving oral sex to giving it. A quarter of a century ago in *The Joy of Sex,* Alex Comfort mused that 'some girls do and some don't like the man to go all the way and ejaculate (if they love him very much, that may make all the difference, but not always).' As Andy Warhol said in *From A to B and Back Again,* 'Everybody I know has a different idea of love. One girl I knew said, "I knew he loved me when he didn't come in my mouth".'

There are a great many women, though, who enjoy fellatio, and John Updike rhapsodizes about them. In one of his poems, he muses about a room full of 'clean secretaries'; each takes a lover's 'fountain' into her mouth. She swallows the seed and her insides 'flower into landscapes'. A pretty picture.

Disapproval of fellatio, however, has a long history. In *Western Sexuality*, Philippe Ariès and André Bejin report that in Greece and Rome, 'There was one type of sexual behaviour which was absolutely disgraceful. Fellatio was a very dirty word.' The objection was political, though, not moral. 'The passive role in fellatio', explains the historian James Brundage in *Law, Sex and Christian Society,* was 'strongly disapproved of' because of 'what was felt to be the incongruity of a free man acting the role customarily assigned to a slave or a servant boy.'

Such historical niceties do not trouble the British novelist Alan Hollinghurst. Anyway, in this scene from his 1993 novel *The Folding Star,* it is hard to know quite which one is the passive partner: 'I went down and nosed and kissed his balls through the sleek black nothing of his swimming shorts, and lifted them on my tongue and let them drop . . . I tugged his balls free with my lips and tongue and little careful cat–nips of the teeth . . . I helped him from the fleeting encumbrance of the shorts.' He lay down on the sun-bed. 'I came after on my knees and licked and pulled and sucked on his balls [while he] yanked in the steady piston of his fist. [Then] he was choking both balls into my mouth to swallow on as he came.'

Courting albatross toss their heads and snap their bills. Between bouts of nodding and bowing, they rub their bills together. Flirting baboons show their interest by smacking their lips. But interspecies kisses are rare. Once, when Dian Fossey just happened to be peeking out of the window of her Rwandan cabin, she witnessed a greeting more likely in a Walt Disney movie. Most of Fossey's hens, of which there were many, were tiptoeing toward a young antelope who had strayed into the camp. Equally curious, the bushbuck was strolling toward them. 'Each chicken then made a beak-to-nose contact with the bushbuck as both species satisfied their undisguised interest in each other.' The birth of love, or merely a kiss of greeting by the hens?

One can read a great deal into nature. To Havelock Ellis, 'The caressing of the antennae practiced by snails and various insects during sexual intercourse is of the nature of a kiss.'

The line from the baby to the beloved is not much in doubt. Long before Freud recognized that our mother's nipple and lips prepare us for our lover's lips, the biblical Song of Songs had made the equation: 'Thy lips, O my spouse, drip as the honeycomb: honey and milk are under your tongue.' Children are still kiss-fed on the banks of the Orinoco. And lovers everywhere take food from each other's mouths.

In Lucy Taylor's erotic short story 'Baubo's Kiss', an Oxford classics student under the spell of a Greek island retraces some of the steps of our earliest experiences of the continuum:

A boy, barely beyond his teens, watched her with a rapt and avid gaze, wetting the corners of his mouth with a tongue made sopping by desire. Mira danced to his side. She took him by his thick black hair and buried his face between her breasts, each one of which was easily the size of the boy's head. She let him suckle, leaving her nipples silvery with saliva, then pushed his head down and hoisted up her skirt and straddled him. His tongue knew dances of its own, quick, darting strumming motions and deep, luxurious slurps and she opened up her folds to him and took his tongue in like a raw pink fetus seeking reentry to its fleshy nest.

The journey along the kiss continuum is one that each of us has been destined to take. It is not like a non-stop flight from London to New York, not a linear journey at all. Nor is it just an odyssey of desire. Its ports are also friendship, affection; religion, familial love, Proustian or not. Kissing games, a ritual of youth, are virtual reality games, preps for the big occasion, but when the first erotic kiss comes, it is usually memorable. Mohammed Ali fainted after his.

It was by kisses, remember, that lovers' souls were exchanged and witches' souls were stolen by the devil, as souls still are by movie vampires. Today, a soul kiss (tongue-kiss) has little to do with souls except in the way Flaubert means here: 'He gave her one of those kisses into which one puts all one's soul.'

A meaningful kiss, though, can be bodiless. In *The Scarlet Pimpernel*, the hero must hide his love from the heroine, but when she turns away, he kisses the ground her skirts have brushed: 'He was a man madly, blindly, passionately in love, and as soon as her light footsteps had died away within the house, he knelt down upon the terrace steps, and in the very madness of love he kissed one by one the places where her small foot had trodden.' This is the sort of thing, I suppose, that Roger Scruton means. Or Judith Kazantzis' fine lines in 'With Love, January':

> They are stretching out like shadows,
> some of these nights. The love whose skirts
> you in your last letter kissed,
> I lift them for you.

But kissing at one remove, the fantasy, in both these instances is intended to lead to something physical. In the *Kama Sutra*, when one kisses the reflection of the loved one in a mirror, in water, or on a wall, it is called a 'kiss of showing the intention'.

Kissing has little primacy if you look at sex merely as a quick means to an orgasm; in which case, masturbation is the most efficient and certain of means. Kissing is also minimized if you look at sex merely as a means of producing offspring. This view, the choice of centuries, has caused rather more harm and less pleasure than masturbation. It is with sensuality that kissing assumes importance. Is kissing an evolutionary advance? Or is it an accident that the two most intelligent of the primates – the humans and the bonobos – are champion kissers?

In ancient Egypt, where the same word could mean 'kiss' or 'eat', Cleopatra and her compatriots may have had some interesting misunderstandings. The connection between food and kissing, as between food and sex generally, which been made by Freud and by ethologists, has also been made by many ancient peoples.

A Babylonian hymn written more than 1500 years before Christ, long before Cleopatra dallied with Mark Antony, begins what was to be a centuries-long association of kissing and food. The lips of the voluptuous goddess of love Ishtar are a source of sweetness and life: 'In lips she is sweet; life is in her mouth.' The Babylonians seem to have known, as we do, that women have two sets of lips.

In a way that oral sex usually isn't, however, and coital sex isn't always, the kiss is reciprocal. In the erotics of kissing mutuality is probably instinctive; quite of its own volition it becomes the game. In the optimal kiss desire becomes physically and emotionally mutual. Reciprocal pleasure is a sine qua non. Desire need not dawn in both lovers at the same time, so long as both do experience the sunlight. Even in the dark.

One can kiss to orgasm, or one can just keep kissing an kissing and kissing. Biologically, in the act of kissing two people communicate as equals, mouth to mouth, tongue to tongue. The other is the other, but also the same. It feels close. *Intimus,* innermost. In anatomy, indeed, may be intimacy.

In *Troilus and Cressida*, she asks, 'In kissing, do you render or receive?' The answer is: both. Kissing blurs the distinction between giving and taking. In kissing one feeds both the other and oneself. 'A kiss is worth nothing until it is divided between two,' says the Gypsy proverb. In kissing one devours without devouring. What this means, really, is that kissing can be a way of having your cake and eating it too, magically, without slaking desire.

NOTES

19 **a mere 6.4 calories**: June
M. Reinisch with Ruth
Beasley, *The Kinsey Institute
New Report on Sex*, p. 77.
Others estimate 150 calories
per steamy session, about as
much as a fifteen-minute
swim.

19 **about 150 at orgasm**:
during the plateau phase of
excitement, men's heart rates
of 100–75 have been
observed. Reinisch, op. cit.,
p. 80. See also William H.
Masters and Virginia
Johnson, *Human Sexual
Response*.

20 **Annabelle Dytham**: the
Royal Society Exhibition on
New Frontiers in Science, 16
and 17 June 1993, showed her
and McGrouther's project, 'A

simple kiss? – An anatomical
study of the moving human
lips'. I interviewed Dytham
some months later.

20 **Gus McGrouther**: see
preceding note. My initial
interview with him in 1993
was followed up in December
1995.

23 **'I hadn't told anyone'**:
Marjorie Shostak, *Nisa: The
Life and Words of a !Kung
Woman*, p. 2.

24 **Sheila Kitzinger**: *The
Experience of Breastfeeding*.

27 **open instincts**: Mary
Midgley explains this very
well in *Beast and Man: The
Roots of Human Nature*, p. 52.

28 **'Sometimes Adrienne'**:
Colette, *My Mother's House
and Sido*.

29 **Liebowitz**: M. R. Liebowitz, *The Chemistry of Love*. Cited in Helen Fisher, *Anatomy of Love*, p. 53.

32 **A medieval manuscript**: cited in Eibl-Eibesfeldt and Gonzales-Crussi's *On the Nature of Things Erotic* makes much of this.

32 **'Strangers would not'**: 'Tony Parsons' Week' in the *Sunday Telegraph*, 11 July 1993.

33 **'Gestures,' explains one**: in Jan Bremmer and Herman Roodenburg, eds., *A Cultural History of Gesture*, p. 133.

33 **Trobriand**: Bronislaw Malinowski, *The Sexual Life of Savages*, p. 280.

36 **Tunisian sheik**: Umar Ibn Muhammed al-Nefzawi. The book was discovered in Algeria in the nineteenth century by a French army officer. The French writer Guy de Maupassant applauded it. The Orientalist Richard Burton translated it into English in 1886.

36 **'They grip'**: Dryden's famous translation.

38 **87 per cent**: study by William Janoviak and Edward Fischer cited by Helen Fisher. op. cit., p. 164. In December 1992 a report to the first ever session on the anthropology of romance at an annual American Anthropological Association meeting.

44 **'Under the pressure'**: 'The Case of Miss Lucie R', published in 1895, one of the *Selected Papers on Hysteria*, is available in English in both editions listed in the bibliography. This translation is my own, done with Julia Pascal.

46 **Kate Millett**: *Sexual Politics*, p. 183.

47 **'As a matter of fact'**: 'The Sexual Enlightenment of Children', in Sigmund Freud, *Penguin Freud Library*, p. 175.

47 **'No one who'**: *Three Essays on Sexuality* (1905), in Sigmund Freud, *Penguin Freud Library*, vol. 7, p. 98.

48 **pleasure: 'His mother'**: *Three Essays*, op. cit., p. 145.

48 **'the nursing couple'**: the psychiatrist D. W. Winnicott used the term in his famous paper on 'primary maternal pre-occupation', 1956.

48 **'By and by'**: Naomi Mitchison, *The Corn King and the Spring Queen*, 1931, cited in Margaret Reynolds, *Erotica*, p. 270.

50 **'It's a pity'**: *Three Essays*, op. cit., p. 98.

51 **'sat down upon'**: James Boswell, *The Journal of a Tour to the Hebrides, with Samuel Johnson, LL.D.*, p. 336. Boswell reports: 'One of the married ladies . . . sat down upon Dr. Johnson's knee, and,

being encouraged by some of the company, put her hands round his neck, and kissed him. – Do it again [said he], and let us see who will tire first.'

52 **the plight of the rake**: Rollo May, *Love and Will*, p. 56.

54 **'My sole consolation'**: *À la recherche du temps perdu*, vol. 1, p. 13.

58 **mother and bride**: this really is the theology of the period. See Armstrong or Warner for good discussions.

62 **Writers continue**: the charge is repeated in passing in Matt Ridley's *The Red Queen: Sex and the Evolution of Human Nature*.

65 **'When I got'**: Farley Mowat, *Woman in the Mists*, p. 286.

66 **Upsuck Hypothesis**: explained to me by Louise Barrett of the University of Liverpool. The timing in relation to male orgasm is critical; maximum sperm retention is associated with climaxes of zero to one minute after the male ejaculates. Barrett refuted the Pole Ax hypothesis which I had rather liked – that a woman basking in the afterglow of orgasm retains more sperm because she doesn't jump up quickly; orgasm during sex does not

increase the number of sperm retained.

67 **'in face-to-face coitus'**: Fisher, op. cit., p. 182.

67 **cats to cattle**: explained to me by Louise Barrett of the University of Liverpool, mentioning Ford and Beach, 1953, for cats; Hartman, 1957, for cattle: Evans, 1933, for dogs; and Allen and Lenor, 1981. Fisher cites more, op. cit., p. 340. See Simon LeVay, *The Sexual Brain*, for a succinct account of lordosis.

69 **San Diego Zoo**: F. B. de Waal, *Chimpanzee Politics*, p. 199.

70 **'The initiation of copulation'**: Jane Goodall, *The Chimpanzees of Gombe*, p. 484.

70 **M. K. Termerlin**: cited in Goodall, op. cit.

73 **'After a while'**: Shostak, op. cit.

74 **Most divorces**: this computation is by Helen Fisher, op. cit.

77 **Labé**: in *Elegies et Sonnets*.

80 **'But by the fourth century AD'**: Mary R. Lefkowitz, *Women in Greek Myth*.

81 **'She flung herself'**: cited in Jane Mills, *Bloomsbury Guide to Erotic Literature*.

83 **William Acton's textbook**: cited in John Elsom, *Erotic Theatre*, p. 20.

87 **thirteenth**: possibly late twelfth century. Francis claimed to be kissing Lady Poverty.

88 **'Rejoice, mother'**: Gustave Flaubert, *Oeuvres, La legend de Saint Julian Hospitalier*, vol. 2, p. 648.

90 **Pope Gregory**: cited in Lawrence Osborne, *The Poisoned Embrace*. His discussion of this period is interesting. See also Karen Armstrong.

92 **variant edition**: cited in George Painter, *Proust*.

93 **'I think of your love'**: cited in Jane Mills, op. cit.

101 **'fond smile'**: there is an interesting discussion of their kiss in Roger Scruton's *Sexual Desire*, p. 128. However, here as elsewhere in the book Scruton tries to desexualize sex.

103 *Perceforest* was first printed in 1528, the *Pentamerone* in 1634–6.

104 **'kissed their dear child'**: Iona and Peter Opie provide a very clear discussion of the various versions in *The Classic Fairy Tales*.

105 **'He opened the door'**: Jacob and Wilhelm Grimm, *The Complete Fairy Tales*.

105 **'Princess: Ah!'**: Opie, op. cit.

106 **Bruno Bettelheim**: *The Uses of Enchantment*.

109 **'Ile be a parke'**: *Venus and Adonis*, stanza 39.

109 **'although she loathed'**: the tale is probably best known in Robert Graves' translation of *The Golden Ass* by Apuleius (*c.* 130–80).

110 **Cupid spread his wings**: Apuleius, op. cit.

111 **a perfect prince**: Marina Warner, *From the Beast to the Blonde*.

113 **his father insisted he marry her**: to his biographer David Dimbleby in the famous televised interview.

115 **kissing her husband's big toe**: Jan Bremmer and Roodenburg, Herman, eds., *A Cultural History of Gesture*, p. 139.

115 **Dr Faustus**: Marlowe's play was first performed in 1594.

127 **'In silence we'**: Bram Stoker, *Bram Stoker's Dracula Omnibus*, p. 41.

127 **'All three had'**: Stoker, op. cit., p. 31.

128 **'Friend Arthur'**: Stoker, op. cit., p. 175.

134 **Reynolds**: in an essay in Jay Leyda and Charles Musser, eds., *Before Hollywood: Turn of the Century Film from American Archives*.

144 **the Greek**: Kirk Hughes, 'Framing Judas' in *Semeia*, no. 54, p. 231.

144 **'A man whom the**

Redeemer': Jorge Borges, 'Three Versions of Judas', in *Fictions*, p. 140.

145 **'We would not name'**: cited in Hughes, op. cit., p. 231.

151 **'pattern of submission'**: Jane Goodall, op. cit., p. 360. She describes the method of chimpanzees: 'kissing (with lips pouted forward to barely touch the other or with mouth wide open and pressed against the other)'.

152 **'Strangers take more readily'**: D. W. Winnicott, *The Piggle*, p. 177.

156 **Erasmus**: cited in Jan Bremmer and Herman Roodenburg, eds., *A Cultural History of Gesture*, p. 221.

158 **'Two people'**: Bremmer, op. cit.

161 **'The movies, the movies'**: lyrics from the song 'The Movies Get You Through' in the musical *A Day in Hollywood, A Night in the Ukraine* by Frank Lazarus and Dick Vosburgh, 1980.

174 **'take [Scarlett]'**: Leonard J. Leff, and Jerold Simmons, *The Dame in the Kimono*.

178 **'I told you'**: in Manguel, Alberto, ed., *The Gates of Paradise*.

183 **Schlesinger**: in an interview on 'The Screen Kiss', a Kaleidoscope feature presented by Harriett Gilbert, BBC Radio, 1994.

191 **'Its power derives'**: Simon Wilson, *Tate Gallery: An Illustrated Guide*, p. 150.

193 **'People say I'**: William Rothenstein, *Men and Memories*, vols. 1 & 2.

193 **'Lovers are besotted'**: Judith Cladel, *Rodin*. For more detail see the biographies by Butler and Grunfeld.

199 **'Flo arrives'**: Goodall, op. cit., p. 443.

200 **'one of the most universally-known'**: Taylor, *Great Movie Moments*.

201 **Caroline Islands**: Havelock Ellis, *Studies in the Psychology of Sex*, vol. 4, p. 22.

202 **Luce Irigaray**: *Ce Sexe qui n'en est pas un*.

202 **Camille Paglia**: in *Sexual Personae*, p. 16.

205 **'The caressing of the antennae'**: Ellis, op. cit.

205 **'Baubo's Kiss'**: in Maxim Jakubowski, ed., *The Mammoth Book of Erotica*, p. 506.

206 **'With Love, January'**: in Judith Kazantzis, *Selected Poems, 1977–1992*, p. 187.

BIBLIOGRAPHY

Ableman, Paul, *The Mouth and Oral Sex* (London: Running Man Press, 1969).

Ackerman, Diane, *A Natural History of Love* (New York: Vintage, 1995).

Amis, Martin, *London Fields* (London: Penguin, 1990).

Apuleius, trans. Robert Graves, *The Golden Ass* (London: Penguin, 1985).

Ariès, Philippe and André Bejin, *Western Sexuality* (Oxford: Blackwell, 1985).

Armstrong, Karen, *A History of God* (London: Heinemann, 1993).

Auster, Paul, *Leviathan* (London: Faber, 1992).

Baker, Nicholson, *The Fermata* (London: Chatto, 1994).
Vox (London: Granta, 1991).

Bataille, George, *Eroticism* (London: John Calder, 1957).

Baudrillard, J., *Simulacres et Simulation* (Paris: Galilée, 1981).

Bettelheim, Bruno, *The Uses of Enchantment* (London: Penguin, 1978).

Borges, Jorge, 'Three Versions of Judas', in *Fictions* (London: Calder, 1962).

Boswell, James, *The Journal of a Tour to the Hebrides, with Samuel Johnson, LL.D.* (London: Oxford University Press, 1978).

Bowlby, John, *Attachment and Loss*, vols. 1, 2, 3 (London: Hogarth, 1969, 1973, 1980).

Bremmer, Jan and Roodenburg, Herman, eds., *A Cultural History of Gesture* (Cambridge: Polity Press, 1991).

Bulfinch, Thomas, *Myths of Greece and Rome* (London: Penguin, 1981).

Buss, David M., *The Evolution of Desire* (New York: Basic Books, 1994).

Butler, Ruth, *Rodin: The Shape of Genius* (New Haven: Yale University Press, 1993).

Campbell, Joseph, *The Hero with a Thousand Faces* (London: Paladin, 1988).

Camus, Albert, *The First Man* (London: Hamish Hamilton, 1995).

Chagnon, Napoleon, *Yanomamo* (New York: Holt, Rinehart & Winston, 1977).

Champigneulle, Bernard, *Rodin* (London: Thames & Hudson, 1967).

Cladel, Judith, *Rodin* (London: Kegan Paul, n.d.).

Clark, Ronald W., *Freud* (London: Cape/Weidenfeld, 1980).

Colette, *My Mother's House and Sido* (New York: Farrar, Strauss & Giroux, 1975).

Collett, Peter, *Foreign Bodies* (London: Simon & Schuster, 1993).

Comfort, Alex, *The Joy of Sex* (London: Mitchell Beazley, 1986).

Cooper, Emmanuel, *The Sexual Perspective* (London and New York: Routledge & Kegan Paul, 1986).

Coward, Rosalind, *Female Desire* (London: Palladin, 1984).

Dante Alighieri, *La Divina commedia* (Ulrico Hoepli, 1899).

de Waal, F. B., *Chimpanzee Politics* (New York: Harper and Row, 1982).

'Bonobo Sex and Society', *Scientific American*, March 1995.

Durden-Smith, Jo and de Simone, Diane, *Sex and the Brain* (London: Pan, 1983).

Eibl-Eibesfeldt, Irenaus, *Love and Hate* (London: Methuen, 1971). *Human Ethology* (New York: Aldine, 1989).

Ellis, Havelock, *Studies in the Psychology of Sex*, vol. 4 (Philadelphia: F. A. Davis, 1914).

Elsom, John, *Erotic Theatre* (London: Secker & Warburg, 1973).

Evans, Charles S., *Sleeping Beauty*, Illus. by Arthur Rackham (London: Heinemann, 1972).

Fisher, Helen, *Anatomy of Love* (London: Simon & Schuster, 1992).

Fitzgerald, F. Scott, *The Great Gatsby* (London: Penguin, 1976).

Flaubert, Gustave, *Oeuvres, La legend de Saint Julian Hospitalier*, vol. 2 (Paris: La Pléiade-Gallimard, 1968).

Ford, Clelland and Frank Beach, *Patterns of Sexual Behaviour* (London: Methuen, 1965).

Fossey, Dian, *Gorillas in the Mist* (London: Penguin, 1985).

Foucault, Michel, *The History of Sexuality* (London: Pelican, 1981).

Freud, Sigmund, *Penguin Freud Library*, vols. 1–7 (Harmondsworth: Penguin Books, n. d.).
The Major Works (Chicago: Encyclopedia Britannica, 1952).

Gonzales-Crussi, F., *On the Nature of Things Erotic* (London: Picador, 1988).

Goodall, Jane, *The Chimpanzees of Gombe* (Cambridge, Mass.: Belknap Press, 1986).

Grimm, Jacob and Wilhelm, *The Complete Fairy Tales* (London: Routledge & Kegan Paul, 1975).

Grimm, J. L. C. & W. C., *Grimms' Fairy Tales* (Hertfordshire: Wordsworth Ltd, 1993).

Grunfeld, Frederic, *Rodin* (Oxford: Oxford University Press, 1989).

Hartog, W. G., *The Kiss in English Poetry* (London: A. M. Philpot, 1923).

Haste, Cate, *Rules of Desire: Sex in Britain* (London: Pimlico, 1994).

Henriques, Fernando, *Love in Action* (London: MacGibbon & Kee, 1964).

Hervez, Jean, *Le Baiser* (Paris: Bibliothèque des Cureiux, 1923).

Hollinghurst, Alan, *The Folding Star* (London: Vintage, 1995).

Howlett, Jane and Rod Mengham, eds., *The Violent Muse* (Manchester: Manchester University Press, 1994).

Hughes, Kirk, T., 'Framing Judas' in *Semeia*, no. 54 (Philadelphia: University of Pennsylvania, 1991).

Irigaray, Luce, *Ce Sexe qui n'en est pas un* (Paris: Les Editions de Minuit, 1977).

Jakubowski, Maxim, ed., *The Mammoth Book of Erotica* (London: BCA, 1994).

James, Henry, *The Portrait of a Lady*, Norton Critical Edition (New York: Norton).

Jones, James, *From Here to Eternity* (London: Collins, 1952).

Jung, C. G., *Four Archetypes* (London: Routledge & Kegan Paul, 1972).

Kazantzis, Judith, *Selected Poems, 1977–1992* (London: Sinclair-Stevenson, 1995).

Kendon, Adam, et al., eds., *Organization of Behaviour in Face-to-Face Interaction* (The Hague: Mouton, 1975).
Conducting Interaction (Cambridge and New York: Cambridge University Press, 1990).

Khatchadourian, Herant, *Biological Aspects of Human Sexuality*, 3rd edn (New York: Holt, Rinehart & Winston, 1987).

Kinsey, A. C., et al., *Sexual Behaviour in the Human Male* (Philadelphia: W. B. Saunders, 1948).
Sexual Behaviour in the Human

Female (Philadelphia: W. B. Saunders, 1953).

Kitzinger, Sheila, The Experience of Breastfeeding (London: Penguin, 1987).

Kundera, Milan, Laughable Loves (London: John Murray, 1978).

Labé, Louise, Elegies et Sonnets (Paris: Baudouin, n. d.).

Laplanche, J. and J. B. Pontalis, The Language of Psychoanalysis (London: Hogarth Press, 1983).

Laurent, Monique, Rodin (London: David & Jenkins, 1988).

Leff, Leonard J. and Jerold Simmons, The Dame in the Kimono (London: Weidenfeld & Nicolson, 1990).

Lefkowitz, Mary R., Women in Greek Myth (London: Duckworth, 1986).

Leyda, Jay and Charles Musser, eds., Before Hollywood: Turn of the Century Film from American Archives (New York: American Federation of Arts, 1986).

LeVay, Simon, The Sexual Brain (Cambridge, Mass.: MIT Press, 1993).

Lucie-Smith, Edward, Sexuality in Western Art (London: Thames & Hudson, 1991).

Maccoby, Hyam, Judas Iscariot and the Myth of Jewish Evil (New York: Free Press, 1992).

Malinowski, Bronislaw, The Sexual Life of Savages (London: Routledge, 1932).

Manguel, Alberto, ed., The Gates of Paradise (London: Flamingo, 1993).

Masters, William H. and Virginia Johnson, Human Sexual Response (Boston: Little, Brown, 1966).

May, Rollo, Love and Will (London: Souvenir Press, 1969).

Meister, Robert, ed., A Literary Guide to Seduction (London: Elek, 1963).

Michael, Robert T., et al., Sex in America (Boston: Little, Brown, 1994).

Midgley, Mary, Beast and Man: The Roots of Human Nature (Hassocks: Harvester Press, 1979).

Millett, Kate, Sexual Politics (London: Abacus, 1972).

Mills, Jane, Bloomsbury Guide to Erotic Literature (London: Bloomsbury, 1993).

Mitchell, Margaret, Gone With the Wind (London: Macmillan, 1988).

Moir, Anne and David Jessel, Brain Sex (London: Mandarin, 1989).

Moore, Brian, The Statement (London: Bloomsbury, 1995)

Morris, Desmond, Babywatching (London: Cape, 1991).
The Naked Ape Trilogy (London: Cape, 1994).

Mowat, Farley, Woman in the Mists (London: Macdonald, 1988).

Nefzawi, Shaykh, trans. by Richard Burton, The Perfumed

Garden (London: Grafton, 1990).

Opie, Iona and Peter, *The Classic Fairy Tales* (London and New York: Oxford University Press, 1974).

Orczy, Baroness, *The Scarlet Pimpernel* (London: Hodder & Stoughton, 1961).

Osborne, Lawrence, *The Poisoned Embrace* (London: Bloomsbury, 1993).

Paglia, Camille, *Sexual Personae* (London: Penguin, 1991).

Painter, George, *Marcel Proust*, 2 vols. (London: Chatto, 1959 and 1965).

Parker, Derek, *An Anthology of Erotic Verse* (London: Book Club Associates, 1980).

Pascall, Jeremy and Clyde Jeavons, *Sex in the Movies* (London: Hamlyn, 1975).

Paz, Octavio, *The Double Flame* (New York: Harcourt Brace, 1995).

Perella, Nicholas James, *The Kiss: Sacred and Profane* (Berkeley: University of California Press, 1969).

Phillips, Adam, *On Kissing, Tickling, and Being Bored* (London: Faber, 1993).

Prost, Antoine and Gérard Vincent, eds., *A History of Private Life*, vol. v (Cambridge, Mass.: Belknap Press, 1991).

Proust, Marcel, *À la recherche du temps perdu*, vol. 1 (Paris: La Pléiade-Gallimard, 1968).

Reinisch, June M., with Ruth Beasley, *The Kinsey Institute New Report on Sex* (London: Penguin, 1990).

Reynolds, Margaret, *Erotica* (London: Pandora, 1990).

Rich, Adrienne, *The Dream of a Common Language* (New York: W. W Norton, 1978).

Ridley, Matt, *The Red Queen: Sex and the Evolution of Human Nature* (London: Penguin, 1993).

Rothenstein, William, *Men and Memories*, vols. 1 & 2 (London: Faber, 1931, 1932).

Rycroft, Charles, *A Critical Dictionary of Psychoanalysis* (New York: Penguin, 1983).

Sarsby, Jacqueline, *Romantic Love and Society* (Harmondsworth: Penguin, 1983).

Schaffer, Rudolph, *Mothering* (London: Fontana, 1985).

Scruton, Roger, *Sexual Desire* (London: Phoenix, 1986).

Selby, Jr., Hubert, *Last Exit to Brooklyn* (London: Paladin, 1987).

Seth, Vikram, *A Suitable Boy* (London: Phoenix, 1993).

Shakespeare, William, ed. Humphrey Jennings, *Venus and Adonis* (London: Alces Press, 1993).

Shostak, Marjorie, *Nisa: The Life and Words of a !Kung Woman* (London: Allen Lane, 1982).

Sox, David, *Bachelors of Art* (London: Fourth Estate, 1991).

Stevens, Anthony, *Archetype*

(London: Routledge & Kegan Paul, 1982).

Stoker, Bram, *Bram Stoker's Dracula Omnibus* (London: Orion, 1992).

Sunshine, Linda, *Lovers* (London: Virgin, 1992).

Suttie, Ian D., *The Origins of Love and Hate* (London: Free Association Book, 1988).

Symons, Donald, *The Evolution of Human Sexuality* (New York: Oxford University Press, 1979).

Tabori, Lena, *Kisses* (London: Virgin, 1991).

Tannahill, Reay, *Sex in History* (London: Abacus, 1993).

Taylor, John Russell, *Great Movie Moments* (London: Shelton, 1987).

Thomson, Oliver, *A History of Sin* (Edinburgh: Canongate, 1993).

Van de Velde, T., *Ideal Marriage* (London: Heinemann, 1962).

Vatsyayana, trans. Richard Burton, *The Kama Sutra* (London: George Allen & Unwin, 1963).

Wagner, Peter, *Eros Revived* (London: Paladin Grafton Books, 1988).

Warner, Marina, *Alone of All Her Sex* (London: Wiedenfeld & Nicolson, 1976).
From the Beast to the Blonde (London: Chatto & Windus, 1994).

Weldon, Fay, *The Life and Loves of a She-Devil* (London: Hodder & Stoughton, 1983).

Wilson, Simon, *Tate Gallery: An Illustrated Guide* (London: Tate Gallery, 1990).

Windybank, Susan, *Wild Sex* (London: Virgin, 1992).

Winnicott, D. W., *The Piggle* (London: Penguin, 1977).

Woolf, Virginia, *Mrs Dalloway* (London: Hogarth Press, 1990).

Zeldin, Theodore, *An Intimate History of Humanity* (London: Sinclair-Stevenson, 1994).

INDEX

INDEX

Adrianne Blue was born and raised in Washington, D.C. After working in New York in the book publishing industry and as a social worker, she began her writing career, contributing short stories and articles to the *Transatlantic Review*, *The Village Voice*, *Fiction International*, and *Cosmopolitan*. After moving to London in 1977 she became *Time Out*'s literary editor, and continued to contribute to such American publications as *Ms.* and the *Washington Post*. In 1980 she began work at the *Sunday Times* (London), soon becoming Britain's most prominent writer on women's sports. She also served as the newspaper's motorcycle racing correspondent. Since 1990 she has been a full-time author and occasional television commentator on women's athletics. She now lives in London and Provence.